# Bipolar Flames:
# Escaping the New Age and
# Redemption through Christ

## Mallory Beckwith, LPC

# Disclaimer

This book is a memoir. The events are portrayed to the best of the author's memory. It reflects the author's present recollections of experiences over time. Some names, characteristics, and identifying details have been changed to protect the privacy of the people involved. Some dialogue has been recreated.

# Contents

# Dedication

This book is dedicated to Tony, who fought on the front lines to help save people from addiction. Tony was one of God's angels in human form who lived his life in service of others. Without Tony's help, I don't know if I would have made it out of my addiction.

# Acknowledgments

I would like to thank God for putting it on my heart to write this memoir. He gave me the strength to relive my trauma and record what happened so my story can now help others. Thank you to my husband, who helped me navigate a psychotic episode while I was writing about my spiritual trauma for the book. Lastly, thank you to Mom, who supported my mission to write and gave me the opportunity to lay down in green pastures at her ranch when the work became heavy.

# About the Author

Mallory Beckwith, LPC is a licensed therapist and Christian life coach who helps individuals strengthen their relationship with Jesus and transition out of the New Age. Mallory also helps individuals recover from bipolar disorder, narcissistic abuse, and PTSD in her counseling and life coaching practices. Mallory is very passionate about mental health, Christianity, psychology, entrepreneurship, and writing. Reach out to Mallory at mallorymillerbeckwith@gmail.com if you would like to work with her. She sees clients in Texas, all over the United States and the world. Family members of a loved one who is struggling with bipolar disorder or stuck practicing New Age spirituality are encouraged to reach out to Mallory as well.

He gives power to the weak.

He increases the strength of him who has no might.

Even the youths faint and get weary,

and the young men utterly fall;


but those who wait for Yahweh will renew their strength.

They will mount up with wings like eagles.

They will run, and not be weary.

They will walk, and not faint.

**ISAIAH 40: 29-31**

# PART 1

## Chapter 1

"Mallory, I need to speak with you," demanded Jenny. She was the news director of a local news station in Spokane, Washington, where I was working at the time. Jenny, skinny as a rail with mousy brown hair and olive skin, marched through the newsroom with tension just radiating off of her in every direction. "Stress balls, stress balls," she murmured under her breath. "Meet me in the back!" she shouted.

*I wonder what this is all about.* I was listening to some EDM mix on SoundCloud with my ear muff headphones on. My breath and body reeked of Gold American Spirits. I didn't even bother popping a mint in my mouth or spraying perfume to cover up the smell. My eyeliner was dark and I was feeling moodier by the day working this job. I had been producing the 6 PM news show.

I got up from my desk and saw the assistant news director, Stew, shoot me a look across the hellhole of a newsroom.

Stew and I had a symbiotic relationship. We both had a knack for investigative reporting. Both of us, most recently, broke an investigative piece about a murder crime before any other station or newspaper in the city. He helped me get my hands on the story before any other reporter in the newsroom, too. He told me several times before that I was the best reporter in that newsroom despite the fact I was stuck producing shows for more than half of my time on the job. The other producer had quit. No one else knew how to produce, operate mics, sound, help the technical director in the newsroom, and boss the reporters around except for me. So, I got stuck producing shows. The contract I signed when joining the team said I would be responsible for "stacking the 6 PM." It turned out to be much more work than just "stacking," and I didn't get as much time out in the field.

Assistant news director Stew, news director Jenny, and little news reporter/ "stacker" me were all gathered for a disciplinary meeting in an office at the front of the building.

Jenny slammed both her hands down on the table, frazzled beyond belief. Her emotions were definitely getting the best of her.

"So, what's going on with you?" she asked me with a matter of fact tone. "What's wrong?"

"Ugh…what do you mean I have no idea what you're talking about?" I responded with sass.

No way I was going to be disrespected like that by my boss. No way. I put my sick-it-to-the-man attitude on. I have plenty of practice wearing that attitude. I did not realize it at the time, but I was enduring a dark bipolar episode mixed with early twenties angst.

"You have a bad attitude in this newsroom, and I am not having it," Jenny exclaimed.

"What, Stew? Do you agree with her?" I shot him a look.

"I'm not getting involved in this discussion; I am just here for support," he said with doubt on his face. I knew I was slightly doomed when I could not get solid backup from Stew in this "conversation" or whatever it was.

"I'm not sure if this position is working out for you, Mallory. Forget the 6 PM; you can just go home…NOW!"

"What? I am not going home. I am going to finish the job," I said. Jenny stormed out. As I walked back to my desk and passed by her on the show set, she said, "Just go home," in a taunting way.

No way I was walking out on the job, even with my boss telling me to. I knew she just wanted me to look bad by getting me to leave work early. There was absolutely no healthy communication in that conversation with my news director. She was stressed out for whatever reason, and I was too stubborn to admit I was bitter about producing. In my mind, I needed more time out in the field. As time passed, working in the "stacker" position, I was getting more depressed by the day.

That day I stuck it out and finished the 6 PM show. By 6:45 I was out of the newsroom and went back to my messy apartment. Exhausted, I loaded a fat bowl of marijuana in my fuchsia plastic bong and ripped it hard. The THC got me high, and I finally had some relief from the angst, bitterness, depression, stress, overstimulation and loneliness. One thing I loved about living in Washington was that smoking marijuana was legal.

A physician I worked with described my brain in three ways. I am either addicted to substances, depressed, or creative and sensitive, which helps create more neural transmitters in the brain. The DNA that holds the codes for addiction and depression also holds the codes for creativity and sensitivity. If I'm not actively being creative or helping people by being sensitive, I might have depression (even if I'm not actively using substances). This is because something has to stimulate the receptors in my brain. They can either go empty, and I suffer, or I can stimulate them with creativity and sensitivity. The other option is I use substances to stimulate them.

I sat down and turned on Game of Thrones. I zoned out until I heard my phone ping me. It was a text from a reporter at the station. *Mallory, do you want a reporting opportunity? There has been a major car accident you can cover. If you can get to the station soon, you can go get the story!* Psh, yeah right, not after the day I had. Plus, I was already stoned. I told her I could not make it and passed out.

I woke up the next morning, dreading going to work. I immediately brewed a pot of coffee and walked into my meditation room to check on my pot plant in the closet. In Washington it was legal to grow marijuana plants if you had a medical marijuana license, which I did have. Ghost train wreck was the strain of weed the plant was supposedly producing. I took out my pH balance kit and stabilized the water in a large ball jar. After confirming the pH in the water was balanced, I watered the pot plant. The light hanging from the closet blared down on the plant. It was healthy and growing. I could barely wait for the flowers to bloom.

*Dang I could drink this coffee and haul over to the newsroom for another stupid day, or I could get high and call Rob,* I thought to myself. After yesterday's fiasco with my news director, I was definitely on the verge of quitting. I just had to confirm a few things before I left that hellhole for good.

I ripped a morning bowl and called Rob. "Mornin'," he answered my call after a few rings.

"Rob, what's up? Yesterday, my boss tried to kick me out of the newsroom. I'm on the verge of quitting. Are you ready to launch Green Gardens? After I leave, I can focus on our company full-time!"

"Are you serious? This is such good news. Quit today and we can meet up to get this thing going."

I texted my boss, telling her I was not coming in. I got no response from her. I wasn't in the frame of mind to officially quit but I knew I would have to soon.

Rob was a friend I had met in a yoga class. After the class, I introduced myself to him, and he invited me to hang out and slackline. Rob, who was 6 foot 5 inches tall, had a large fluffy black afro. He frequently messed with it while I was talking to him. It was quite distracting but I thought it was endearing. He thought combing his afro would make it larger. Maybe it did, but in my mind, it did not need to be any bigger. He was clearly dedicated to the process of making it the biggest afro possible.

Each time we hung out we sunk deeper into each other's make-believe worlds. Alone, our psychotic thinking did not make much sense, but together, our delusions grew stronger with each and every conversation we held. We would spend hours together at the park and talk about how we were the reincarnation of Meriwether Lewis and Sacagawea. Because we both felt so connected to the Pacific Northwest and each other, we were sure we both crossed paths in history while exploring this land.

This was something we believed to our very core, not just an inside joke or random thought. We took a day trip to a nearby massive 200-foot waterfall and explored the magnificent canyon it was in. The awe-inspiring scene made us feel even more deeply connected to the Pacific Northwest.

There was no mistake in our minds that we had explored this territory together in a past life. We sat on a hill together on the top of the canyon and lit a joint. The trees all around us were witnessing the return of Meriwether Lewis and Sacagawea. The knots in their trunks were the eyes that saw. Nature celebrated with us upon our glorious return.

When I officially quit my news reporter/ "stacker" job, we fed deeper into each other's delusions. It got so bad to the point that we thought Rob was the incarnate of Jesus and I was the incarnate of Mary Magdalene. We came to the consensus that we bore the burden of being responsible for the 7.4 billion (the number of people on Earth in 2016) people on the planet. It was our job to save everyone's lives or at least try to. How were we going to do that? We weren't quite sure, but I had faith that God had a master plan for both of us.

When Rob was visiting my apartment, I pulled out the journal I had written in while on a 5-day silent retreat when I was a junior in college. In this journal, I wrote love poems to Jesus. It all made sense now. I was in love with Rob, who was actually Jesus, and that is why I wrote these love poems to him when I was on the retreat.

I read the love poems I wrote to Jesus (Rob), and he saw how deep my loyalty was to him. Two hot tears rolled down both of Rob's cheeks. He stood up, wrapped his arms around me, and said, "Thank you."

There were other coincidences that pointed to the fact that Rob was not only the incarnate of Jesus and Meriweather Lewis but also Jimi Hendrix. Rob was a musician and a very good one too. He played the guitar at bars all around town, and performed with a couple different bands. He recorded his own album and I loved the songs on it. The talent he had in this life as Rob was borrowed from his life as Jimi Hendrix.

The reporter in me needed to record this man's history - I mean, come on, he was legendary. I felt so honored to have the opportunity to tell his story. I called my uncle, brimming with excitement to tell him I was going to write the "new bible". Something inside of me still held me back when I wanted to tell him I was spending time with Christ. That little piece of sanity inside of me that was still left. My uncle, who I assume was trying to be polite when I told him, replied, "It's a possibility, Mal!" He had very little context to where I was mentally. His response supported my fantasy of being one of God's prophets.

# Chapter 2

Rob and I grew to be more than friends as we worked on developing Green Gardens. The idea was to start a company where we would help the people who hired us grow their own garden. We frequently discussed whether that "garden" should be a vegetable garden or a closet marijuana pot garden. Legislation gave people the freedom to legally grow marijuana plants at their residence in Washington State if they had a medical marijuana license. I thought this would be the perfect opportunity to help people sustainably grow their own pot plants. Rob mostly wanted to help people grow vegetables, but I convinced him that marijuana plants were the way to go.

We started researching the best materials to purchase for closet marijuana setups, including lights, soil, and pH balance kits. We had the idea to set up 3 Facebook business pages, each with a different theme, and see which one generated the most traction. The first page "Spirit + Plant," was for discussing the spiritual connection you can form with your plant while growing it. The second page, "Growing Medical Cannabis," was to educate customers on how to successfully grow a marijuana plant. The third page, "Growing Medical Cannabis Legally," shared tips on how to grow marijuana but also added information on the laws around growing.

I reached out to an acquaintance of mine who went to college with me. His name was Derrick Baker and he did web development. I offered to fly him out to Spokane to work with me and Rob to grow the company and create the website to help us sell our setup kits. He helped set up the Facebook pages right away and moved to Spokane in June 2016. Derrick and I had hooked up a couple of times freshman year of college but we never were serious about each other. I failed to leave that little detail out to Rob, but I did not think he would really care anyway. Rob actually trusted Derrick because he helped us get the tech side up and running pretty quickly.

Derrick and I would FaceTime about our vision for the website sometimes when Rob was not around. Derrick was so much more attractive than he was in college when we first met. His hair was brown and long, and his demeanor was so calm and cool. Back in college, he was hyper and very talkative. I was much more relaxed around this new Derrick. Something changed about him- he was more spiritual and also had long hair now. I was much more attracted to this version of him, too.

Rob and I picked Derrick up at the airport together when he flew out. As I drove up to the roundabout, I saw him standing by the curb with a large suitcase. He was wearing tight, black, raw denim ripped jeans, a white T-shirt that read "Permanent Vacation" across the front, black slip-on Birkenstocks, and a bright, colorful tie-dyed bandana around his head. His hair was down and long. He looked hot, even sexier than Rob!

We picked him up and drove off from the airport. Rob started pointing things out about Spokane as we drove through the town back to my apartment. Derrick straight up told Rob, "Thanks, but I don't really care." I don't think he was saying this to be rude; it's just he genuinely was not interested. Derrick, from Los Angeles, was not impressed one bit by Spokane.

All three of us decided it would be best if Derrick moved into Rob's apartment. The only problem was that Rob's extra room was a disaster. There was furniture awkwardly placed, and trash and old books were strewn across the filthy carpet. All three of us spent hours cleaning that room up so it was livable for Derrick. There was a futon in there that Derrick was going to sleep on. Rob's apartment looked 10 times better once his extra room was cleaned up. It made a huge difference. It was for sure, an upgrade.

At this point, I had been avoiding talking to my immediate family and updating them on my life. I knew they would judge me, my business partners, and my dreams to establish Green Gardens and help people grow marijuana. I talked to a few of my family members since I left my news reporter job but I did not speak with my father. I knew he would be very upset about my new path.

I started paying for Rob's rent as a "business expense." I justified doing this in my head because if he and now Derrick did not have a place to live, the business could not take off. Rob had gotten several eviction notices delivered to his apartment so I just went ahead, paid his rent, and took care of the problem.

Rob was not 100% on board with me paying his rent though. He did not like that his now girlfriend/business partner was supporting him financially. One afternoon, when I was driving him back to his apartment from the park, he told me I was trying to manipulate and control him with money by paying his rent. We got into a huge argument. I was so heated I slammed on the gas and started swerving down a residential street. I was driving very recklessly. I snapped back into the present moment and did what I could to calm myself down. Luckily, at this point, we were a block away from his apartment. I dropped him off and left with my heart still beating out of my chest.

I called Rob when I got home. He started getting upset with me again over the phone, saying he never wanted Green Gardens to be a company that helped people grow pot. He wanted to help people grow vegetables. He told me things were not going to work out with the business. When I hung up, it became perfectly clear to me - that if things were not working out in the business, they would not work out in the relationship either. There was only one thing left to do before moving forward - I had to check in with Derrick to see if he still wanted to go in on Green Gardens.

I texted Derrick, and he told me he was still at Rob's. I told him Rob was out and asked him if he still wanted to be a business partner to grow Green Gardens. Derrick was still in. I invited him to move into my meditation room and live with me while we launched. It sucked that Rob and I were breaking up in the business and the relationship, but I still had Derrick. What a blessing!

I picked up Derrick, and we drove across town to my place. He lugged his suitcase up the stairs to my apartment and slapped my butt on the way up. He settled into the meditation room. I confided in Derrick about how I was feeling now that Rob and I were breaking up. I asked Derrick, "So, Rob is not Jesus?" If Rob was Jesus he would have never left my side.

Derrick responded, "Rob is not Jesus; we are all Jesus, Mallory."

That night before bed, I walked into the meditation room to tell Derrick goodnight. He was not lying on the futon but was sprawled out on the floor with his head on a pillow and a blanket over him.

"What are you doing on the floor, Derrick?" I asked.

"I sleep on the floor; it's better for your skeletal structure," he replied. I thought this was a little funny, but at least he wasn't claiming to be Jimmy Hendrix.

I was very spiritually confused after breaking up with Rob, who for months at that point, I believed was Jesus. I slipped into having mixed episodes as my undiagnosed bipolar disorder progressed. The breakup was a trigger for me. I threw myself harder into setting up the business. I was very elevated, high-strung, and manic (although I did not know it at the time) while working out the logistics. I hired a lawyer to set up the LLC and met with him multiple times, helped Derrick design the website, researched and ordered 10 set up kits to help people start growing marijuana, found a space for us to store our materials, designed business cards, and threw money into marketing the three Facebook pages we set up.

I was working hard during the day but at night, I would crash. I bought Derrick a $700 slime-green marijuana dab rig and a torch. I started smoking "dabs" (slang for concentrated cannabis oil) at night with Derrick to numb the depressive crashes. Although very potent, concentrated cannabis oil was legal to smoke in Washington State. One night, I locked myself in my room, dropped down to my knees and prayed to God.

"Lord, I do not know what is going on. I thought Rob was Jesus but now I am just confused. I will do ANYTHING to walk the path you have set out for me. Please just show me the way."

# Chapter 3

As Derrick and I launched the business together, we grew very close. Our energy levels seemed to match and we both loved to get high. Derrick would always go further than me when we took dabs. We were working very closely together, living together, and were attracted to each other, so naturally, we became physically intimate. Being with Derrick felt very different, and our connection was something I'd never experienced before with any other past boyfriend or hook-up. We had so much energy we would stay up all night long having sex. All of a sudden, 7 AM would roll around in a blink of an eye. I did not get a wink of sleep, yet I still was not tired at all! This was not normal. Even in my confused head, I still knew what we were experiencing was not just regular sex.

Later, I would find out this was manic sex.

At the time, I knew nothing about bipolar disorder, mania, delusions, or depression. I knew I was not stable though; something inside of me felt very off. One evening, I took a big dab rip off Derrick's rig and remembered thinking to myself. *Oh, this is what it's like to go insane.* All Derrick could say was, "It's lit!" and he would start dying laughing to himself. That insane laugh made a lasting impression on me.

Getting high was nothing new to me. Smoking alone never made me psychotic. My bipolar disorder was triggered at the age of 23 which induced my psychosis. The marijuana did not make it better though. I did began using marijuana more heavily, however, as a way to cope with my episodes.

I never had this much energy before in my entire life, but at the same time, I had never felt so down. I would listen to music and start sobbing when the lyrics hit me. This was not normal either. Music always moved me but did not make me sob like a little baby. Even with all this insanity and emotional turmoil, we still launched our website and sold our first kit. We bought tickets to see Crystal Castles in Portland and Seattle and just so happened to install our first grow closet set up the day we left for Portland.

We arrived at our customer's house and installed the light. Our customers, Casey and Lane, were so excited. Derrick and I were head over heels for each other at this point and could not keep our hands off each other. We talked to each other using psychotic expressions and joked around while setting up the light. Lane made a comment to us with a huge grin on his face, "Where are you two? Y'all are out of this world!" I remembered his comment so vividly because I truly felt like at some point, my spirit had traveled to Saturn and back. I definitely was not "all there," and neither was Derrick.

After installing our first customer's closet marijuana grow set up, we hit the road to Portland, which was a 5.5-hour drive west of Spokane. It was a gorgeous drive along the Columbia River Gorge. We drove through Hood River, Oregon, where we saw windsurfers cruising down the 1.5-mile-wide river. We drove along thick forests and saw large mountain peaks as we headed west. The air was fresh and it was a sunny, clear day. When we stopped to get gas, I got out of the car. I felt the warm breeze whip through my hair. Derrick and I had an electric pull toward each other and held each other tight as the gas pump with the wind blowing around us.

We had one stop to make on our way to see Crystal Castles. We arrived at a grow warehouse to get a private tour. I had reached out to this business and told them about our little start-up, Green Gardens, and asked them to check out their grow house to learn more about the legal marijuana business.

We pulled up and were immediately greeted by an employee who showed us where to park. Walking in, I was impressed with how organized everything was.

The employee who gave us the tour shared, "Keeping the grow house clean and organized is so important. Right now, this is actually the most unorganized it's ever been." *This is unorganized?* I thought to myself. "Take notes for Green Gardens," Derrick whispered in my ear.

Everything looked perfectly placed. He gave us a peak of the main grow room filled with rows and rows of budding marijuana plants. Grow lights shining with a purple tint hung down from the ceiling over the buds, powering them with energy.

After checking out the grow room, the employee brought us to his office, which was also neat and tidy. He gave us some swag including two hats and two shirts. On top of that, he gave us a few grams of ready-to-smoke buds packaged in tiny zip locks. I was so excited to get this swag and threw on my new hat right away. It was so dope.

We left pretty quickly after getting our swag - Crystal Castles was going live in about an hour. We drove to our hotel, parked my Subaru, and headed up to our room. I set my bag down and started getting ready for the show. I put on my red leotard with Native American cave drawings on it and a black leather skirt with black boots. I needed to wear thick eyeliner for this outfit to work. I drew it on and finished applying my makeup with a coat of red lipstick to match my red leotard from American Apparel.

Derrick, who quickly got dressed while I was getting ready, asked me if I was ready to go.

We looked at the time, and it was 8:30 PM. Doors at the club opened at 8:00. We thought if we got there by 9:00 that would surely be enough time to see Crystal Castles take the stage.

We walked to the club and got there right at 9:00. When we got to the dance floor we saw Crystal Castles was already on stage performing one of their more popular songs, "Not in Love." Derrick and I, still in a psychotic frame of mind, were a bit confused as to why "not in love" was playing when we were clearly so deeply in love. We started to get worried and concerned…were we not in love? At this point, we were both experiencing apophenia, which is when someone draws meaningful connections between completely unrelated things. We were applying the lyrics Crystal Castles was singing very literally to our relationship. Apophenia commonly occurs in the mind of someone with bipolar disorder who is experiencing psychosis.

Derrick had a brilliant (psychotic) thought pop up in his head that he shared with me, and it made me feel loads better. "We are "knot" in love, Mallory!" he exclaimed while pointing to his ring finger.

IT ALL MADE SENSE!

As we had this epiphany together that we were meant to get married because we were "knot" in love, the song ended and Crystal Castles left the stage.

"What, it's over?" I asked Derrick. I was so confused why Crystal Castles was leaving!

Everyone left the club. It was only 9:15 and everyone was getting out of there. "I guess they went on right when the club opened," said Derrick.

I wanted to go to another club, but Derrick convinced me it would be best to just go back to the hotel room.

We arrived at our room safely and moments later, laid down on the bed. Derrick and I fell asleep. Hours later I heard the sound of alien noises and the sight of Derrick hovering above me, looking at me. *Holy shit there are aliens in the room.* Derrick heard them, too but did not dare open his mouth. He gave me a couple of nods which confirmed he was hearing the same alien noises as me. I sat up and saw a piece of art in front of me that was a steep staircase. *Did I just climb the stairway to heaven?* I asked myself. In my head, I could understand the aliens. They were telling me I needed to urgently get rid of my ego. Not exactly sure what that meant but I knew that's what they were saying.

I fell asleep again and woke up again the next morning. "Remember the aliens last night, Derrick? I could understand what they were saying."

"Yes," he replied with the bleakest expression ever. "Check behind your ears." "For what?" I asked.

I looked behind my ear in the mirror, and I saw a small slit that Derrick pointed out. "You were able to interpret what they were saying because they put a piece of tech in you to help you translate."

I was full of mixed emotions. I was concerned to see a slit behind my ear that I had never noticed before in my entire life, I was amazed aliens had visited us last night and I had quite possibly entered heaven, and I was also excited to have the realization that Derrick and I were going to get married because we were "knot" in love!

"Do you remember doing all of those complex yoga poses last night, Mallory?" Derrick asked. "You were doing some crazy yoga before the aliens visited."

"Hmm no I don't remember doing yoga; I just remember waking up to the aliens."

I pondered on what happened last night but decided not to dwell on it because we needed to get to Seattle to see Crystal Castles again, and this time we were showing up to the venue on time to see the whole show!

# Chapter 4

We drove from Portland to Seattle that morning, which was roughly a three-hour drive. I let Derrick drive, and I helped him navigate the highways. It took quite a bit of mental energy to get there. We checked into our hotel when we arrived. There was a massive spotted pig statue in the lobby. I remember thinking it was very cute. We got ready for the next show. This time, I cared less about my appearance. Black sweatpants and a sweatshirt that had an infinity sign on it that read "Forever Young" on it is what I wore. We took the elevator down from our floor, and hopped into a cab to the block party where Crystal Castles was playing.

The concert was a blur. I danced a lot and so did Derrick. At one point, I danced with another random person standing next to me solely by making funky hand gestures, and Derrick got upset because I "threw energy at him."

When Crystal Castles wrapped up, we did not stay for the rest of the block party. Instead, we went back to the hotel room, where we locked ourselves up for 3 days.

Things kept getting stranger and stranger in that room. We lay in bed for hours, not talking. Derrick played Kid Cudi's entire album "Speeding Bullet to Heaven" on his iPhone speakers, the darkest and most depressing one that Kid Cudi ever recorded. At one point, I came down with a horrible stomach ache. The vibes in that hotel room were psychotic, to say the least. I thought some dark energy was attaching itself to me, but who really knows.

The hotel called us a couple of times over the three days and asked, "Will you be checking out today?" I would reply, "Give us one more day." After the third or fourth time they called, I decided we had to get out of there. We had not eaten or interacted with the outside world for a while.

"We are getting out of here," I told Derrick. He wasn't too keen on leaving, but he had no choice. We got into the car and I let Derrick drive.

On the road from Seattle to Spokane, Derrick started having a panic attack behind the wheel. "There are too many numbers; look at all the numbers!" He screamed while pointing to the dashboard. He was losing control of the vehicle.

"PULL OVER!" I shouted. "NOW!" Derrick listened to me and abruptly swerved to the side of the road, stopping and putting the car in park.

"GET OUT OF THE CAR!" I yelled.

We both got out of the car, and I walked to the driver's seat, and he got into the passenger's seat. I was by no means stable but I wasn't panicking about numbers either. Somehow, I got us back to the apartment.

Things weren't going too well for either of us. I managed to call my cousin when we got home. I told her how Derrick and I communicated with aliens when we were in Portland. She asked me so many questions. At one point, I got too overwhelmed to hold the conversation, cut her off, and hung up the phone.

We settled back into the apartment and did not leave for 10 days straight. During these 10 days, I was mentally unstable, specifically manic and psychotic, which led me to search for answers and try to figure out the meaning of life. Neurons in the brains of individuals experiencing mania are very excitable. This means these cells in a bipolar person's brain are highly aroused and sensitive to stimuli. I was on high alert and felt multiple dark presences in that apartment during those 10 days.

I was not actively taking substances at the time. The last time I smoked marijuana was back in Seattle. However, in this manic and psychotic state, I would have one hallucination after the other. I left my body numerous times, spent hours meditating, read psychotic articles on the internet, and cooked a bowl of quinoa every few days. One night, I disassociated so hard that my spirit went into outer space, leaving my body behind. This was the most peace and serenity I had ever felt in my life up to this point. There was darkness all around me, but bright stars lit up the night sky. I floated without a care in the world, melding into my surroundings, but I did come back down to my body lying on my bed. Although the experience was peaceful while I was out of my body, it was traumatic coming back down. I was confused about this experience and wondered what really happened.

The most intense hallucination happened when I was standing in my meditation room, staring at my orange and red beaded mandala hanging high on the wall. Derrick was sitting next to me holding a large chunk of kyanite, which is a mineral that is blue and iridescent. He was pointing it directly at me, and I could feel the energy from the stone.

Suddenly, the mandala swirled open. The center stone was no longer there and in its place was an energy vortex. I felt a powerful wave of electric energy flow up my spine through my body to the top of my head. I believed I was going to die at this point - I whispered goodbye to my family and felt my soul come pouring out through the top of my crown into the mandala vortex, which I thought was a portal to the open universe.

My body was drenched in sweat, and my hands were shaking. I grabbed a water bottle on the floor and poured the whole thing on my head to cool off. What in the world had just happened? At the time, I was very confused. My soul just left my body, so why was I still here in this room? Was I still alive?

Little did I know, I had just experienced a kundalini awakening. In the Hindu faith, this is when the primal energy or "serpent energy" wrapped around the base of the spine rises up the body along the spine through the chakras (energy centers in the body), ultimately activating the crown chakra, which is energy center above the head. According to the Hindu faith, the energy rises, and the crown awakens, thus the individual experiencing it reaches a new level of cosmic awareness.

In the Eastern traditions an individual practicing to have a kundalini awakening has a guru who carefully helps them raise this primal energy step by step. But spontaneous kundalini awakening can be triggered by substance use, fasting, trauma, or when the mind is under extreme stress. Kundalini is extremely dangerous and can cause one to feel completely disconnected from oneself, have hallucinations, intense feelings of being overwhelmed, drastic mood swings, confusion, grandiosity, going into trance-like states, and heightened sensitivity, to name a few of the symptoms. These symptoms, which I was already experiencing due to my undiagnosed bipolar disorder, worsened my condition drastically.

I personally think any energy force with the potential to be so dangerous, regardless if it can be awakened in a controlled way under a guru, comes from Satan himself.

I became extremely psychotic and gravely confused after my kundalini activated. I was a severely mentally ill and suffering from psychosis, and I believe Satan took advantage of my pitiful situation by activating the kundalini and making things much worse.

I felt empty inside. The person I used to be was gone; my very essence escaped. This took a few days to accept. I would no longer be the person I used to be from that day forward. I spent a few days meditating on this tragic experience. I was still isolated in my apartment. I had lost a significant amount of weight. Derrick and I were locked up together in what felt like an alternate universe. We weren't answering our phones or keeping contact with the outside world.

One morning, Derrick and I were meditating in the living room. We heard a knock on the door. I opened the door and saw my cousin Eloise standing there. *How was this possible?* I thought to myself. *She lives across the country; why is she showing up at my doorstep?*

"Hey Mallory, what's going on here?" she asked. I felt so confused, embarrassed, and ashamed.

"Come in, we are meditating," I said.

Eloise walked into my apartment and scoped out the area. "How long have y'all been in here?" she asked.

"Not sure, maybe a couple of weeks," I replied.

Derrick kept quiet. He was so deep in his psychosis that he almost forgot how to communicate.

He looked strange. I had shaved his head a few days before. My hair, which was previously long past my shoulders, was now chopped off at my chin. Derrick chopped it off after I shaved his head.

Eloise had a look on her face like she was deeply concerned about what had been going on in this apartment the past few weeks. She must have noticed how gaunt we both were and asked if we wanted to go get some lunch.

The thought of leaving the apartment was anxiety-provoking. We hadn't left in two weeks. Going outside felt risky. But I wanted to act "normal" around my cousin.

"Let us put on some clothes first, then we can head out to lunch," I said. I was wearing a sports bra and shorts. My hair was filthy, and I smelled.

Derrick and I both put on some somewhat presentable clothes. He wore basketball shorts and a T-shirt. We all left the apartment and drove to downtown Spokane, where coincidentally a farmer's market was going on.

We found a cute restaurant to eat at and sat down. This was the most awkward lunch of my life. Derrick and I were both deeply psychotic and detached from reality. Derrick dazed off into the distance while Eloise tried to comprehend the situation. After we ate, we went outside to check out the farmer's market. Derrick dashed off in the opposite direction, and I became concerned. But I was still too interested in the farmers market to start looking for him.

I walked out into the grass and began doing sun salutations. I held my arms long above my head in a mountain pose with my feet hip-width apart on the floor, bowed forward, and jumped back into plank. Next, I pushed up into an upward-facing dog, then a downward-facing dog. I must have looked like a complete weirdo doing them in the middle of the farmers' market. It was a sunny, nice day but no one was doing yoga in the middle of all the booths except me.

I felt highly energized and started exploring. I saw a booth selling gargoyles and felt the impulsive urge to buy one. I impulsively bought the $200 stone figure and my cousin saw me hand over the cash. I asked her to help me bring it to the car; it weighed about 40 pounds.

"Why are you getting this, Mal?" asked Eloise. I could tell my cousin thought this gargoyle was hideous. "Spiritual protection," I replied." "I wonder where Derrick is? Have you seen him?"

After bringing my questionable purchase to the car, I started frantically looking around the farmers market for him. But he was nowhere to be found, and I started to worry. Eloise joined the search. Overwhelmed with fear, thoughts were racing through my head. Why did he run away so quickly after lunch? Was Derrick going to be ok? Even though I knew I was mentally not doing too well, something deep inside of me knew that Derrick was even worse off than I was. He barely even said a word at lunch.

"I don't think we are going to find him, Mallory," said my cousin. "Let's go back to your apartment." A part of me wanted to keep looking but he was long gone at this point. I didn't know what else to do besides get in the car with my cousin and drive back to my apartment.

# Chapter 5

The surge of energy I felt at the farmer's market when I was doing yoga was gone. Feelings of emptiness, fear, and desperation began to creep in. I started crying. I was so upset that Derrick left. Where did he go? Why did he rush off like that? Was he going to be ok?

At this point, Eloise had seen my mood change from high energy and impulsive spending to depression. It was a lot for her to handle on her own. I was rapid cycling in front of her eyes.

I did not know what to do with myself, so I loaded a bowl of marijuana and smoked. This seemed to dull the feelings of depression.

"Your apartment is a mess, Mallory," said Eloise. I was confused because, to me, it looked clean and picked up.

She wiped down the living room table as I enjoyed my high.

Later that evening, I invited Eloise to take a walk on some local nature trails. Getting out was my little nature escape from the small city. I went there to get high, watch the sunset, and swim in a small local creek.

We drove to the trailhead. Once we got there, I felt a burst of energy and started manically running down the trail.

"Wait for me!" Eloise shouted as I sprinted down the trail.

Once I got to a nice private creek bed, I pulled out my pipe, loaded a bowl of marijuana that I had grown myself, and started smoking some more. The sunset looked nice on the edge of the creek.

"Why do you keep smoking?" Eloise asked. "Do you want some?" I offered.

"No, I'm good," she replied.

After the sunset, we walked back to the car and drove back to the apartment. Once inside, Eloise said she was going to take a shower.

"Why is the water not getting warm?" She asked. She realized I had not paid the gas bill. I realized I had not showered in over two weeks.

I began to feel depressed again and began crying. Derrick was still gone; it was dark, and I was worried.

That night, I checked my voicemail and listened to a message from a policeman.

He said, "Hello, this is the Richland Police. I have found Derrick Baker in the middle of the street and he gave me your number and told me to tell you I have him. I am bringing him to the Spokane Hospital. If you need him, you can find him there. Thank you."

"Derrick is in the hospital!" I shouted. "We need to go now!"

Eloise did not want to go on another one of my manic adventures. This was the first time she had ever interacted with Derrick, and she did not seem too thrilled about going on a wild goose chase for my psychotic hippie boyfriend at a hospital. Reluctantly, she got in the car with me and off we went to the hospital to check in with Derrick.

We walked in, and a nurse led us to Derrick's bed. He was extremely disoriented but when he saw me, his face lit up. He said things like, "Boy, did that little duck get me lit," I knew what he was talking about, but he made no sense to the nurses or my cousin. I hugged him and told him how worried I was when he ran off. We clung to each other for support.

The nurses told my cousin. "He is not in a good mental state. And she looks like she could use some help, too."

They must have heard us talking to each other in a way that did not make much sense and realized that we were both detached from reality.

"Come on, Mallory, we need to go. The nurse here is going to take care of Derrick; he needs help right now," my cousin said, pulling me towards the door.

The waterworks began. I sobbed and refused to leave.

"Derrick needs me to stay here with him." I looked at him, and he was so completely out of this world, far from grounded. He did not respond to my emotional sobs.

"We need to go NOW, Mallory." My cousin dragged me out of the hospital room, down the hall and out the door. "Are you ok to drive? We need to get back to your apartment; Derrick is going to be fine here."

"Yes, I can drive." I got behind the wheel and drove off. I looked at my cousin and could tell she immediately regretted the decision to let me drive. But she did not say anything the whole way back.

I was too manic and worried about Derrick to sleep that night. My cousin was exhausted from having to babysit me all day, chase me around the local trails, and watch me shift from high levels of mania to crying spells of depression to having psychotic conversations with Derrick. She passed out on the couch and did not wake up until the morning. I frantically called the hospital over and over again, asking about Derrick. The nurses let me know due to HIPAA they could not answer any of my questions. Somehow, I made it through the night. Right when the sun peeked over the horizon, I decided to drive to the hospital to see Derrick again.

When I got there, I rushed toward Derrick's room. The nurse ran up to me and told me "He is not here anymore."

"Where did he go?" I asked.

"We cannot tell you due to HIPAA," she replied. That was the fifth or sixth time I heard a nurse use that word. I had no idea what it meant but it was stopping me from seeing my baby.

"You need to leave. You cannot be back here," the nurse told me in a stern voice.

I was lost for words. Why wouldn't anyone here at this hospital tell me where he was?

An unfamiliar face walked up to me and whispered to me exactly which psychiatric facility he was at. Bingo! That was the answer I needed. I whispered "Thanks" back and rushed off.

I plugged the psychiatric hospital into my Google Maps and drove off. The moment I arrived, I rushed into the building.

"Hold up, you stop right there," security shouted.

"I am here to get Derrick Baker out!" I shouted back.

The lady at the front desk and the security guard both exchanged a glance. I must have looked crazed, disheveled, and manic. It had been weeks since I showered and days since I slept. It was clearly obvious I had no business storming into this psychiatric hospital and making demands. In fact, I looked like I belonged there myself.

"Mam, we cannot either confirm or deny that this person you are looking for is here."

"WHAT!" I screamed. "I KNOW HE IS HERE! THE LADY AT THE HOSPITAL TOLD ME HE IS HERE."

"Mam, you need to leave immediately," the guard said as he started walking towards me.

"No, I am not leaving until I see Derrick!"

"Ma'am, I am going to have to escort you out." The guard walked me out of the building. I lingered outside for a while. My heart was racing in my chest, I was sweating, and I was upset.

"Oh no, oh no, oh no, oh NO! I am NEVER going to see him again," I yelled. The depression started settling in again.

The security guard walked up to me. "You need to leave the premises immediately."

I had no choice but to get out of there. I was not welcome. I was devastated and could not handle the wave of emotions that washed over me.

I drove back to the apartment, where I found my cousin waking up. It was nearly 8:00 in the morning.

"Your mom and dad are flying in today," she declared. "What?"

"You are not well, Mallory. You are all over the place. Your mood is changing moment to moment, I cannot keep up with you. The conversation you had with Derrick last night made no sense.

One minute, you are crying; the next, you are shouting, doing yoga in public, smoking, and running off on an adventure. You are out of control. Your mom and dad are coming to get you."

My parents showed up at my apartment a few hours later. This was very strange; the two of them divorced but flew all the way out to Spokane from Phoenix to come get me. My behavior became even more erratic when they arrived.

We all went out to eat lunch while I was clearly out of my mind. I told both of my parents that "Mallory is gone now" and that I had seen my own death when the mandala vortex took my soul. After lunch, we walked around for a bit. I started yelling at the top of my lungs, seeing black spots cover the sky and fell back into a yogi backbend.

My parents were lost for words. When we got back to my apartment, I packed a small bag. "We are flying out first thing tomorrow," said my dad.

The next morning, we all went to the airport. Eloise flew back to the East Coast, and my mom, dad, and I flew back to Phoenix. I almost wouldn't board the flight, but my parents convinced me to go.

When we landed, my parents immediately brought me to see a doctor who prescribed me a very powerful pill. My mom made me take it when I got back to her house and boy, did I go out faster than you could blow out a candle. I woke up 24 hours later. I was in bed for a full day.

When I woke up, I realized how long I had been lying there. I was pretty upset that the pill made me sleep for so long. The next couple of days at my mom's house blended together. One day, my aunt showed up at my mom's house with a St. Benedict Key, and I kid you not, five minutes later, my mom's catholic friend showed up with a St. Benedict pendant. The pendant was for my mom, and the key was for me. My aunt and my mom's friend had no clue that the other was bringing a St. Benedict gift. In my mind, this was a very good sign that St. Benedict was here to help. I later found out that the key had an exorcism against Satan written on it.

The one thing I do clearly remember was when my cousin flew back into town from the East Coast and teamed up with my aunt to trick me into going to a mental hospital. I spent about three days in the mental unit, where I met a Vietnam War vet who claimed that he beheaded people in the war while in the Vietnamese jungle. I also made friends with a young Indian lady who wanted to kill herself. Great company, right? The veteran scared me, but I grew close to the Indian lady. I told her about my plans to go back to Spokane when I was released from the hospital, and she offered to drive me there.

When I got out of the mental unit, my mom picked me up with a big smile on her face and drove me back to her house. A couple of days later my dad picked me up from my mom's house with my little brother. I found it odd that my mom was very concerned with what I was wearing that day. But when I got to my dad's house, it all made sense.

There were about 7 cars parked in the driveway. My stomach dropped. This must be an intervention. Somehow, I knew. My brother encouraged me to go inside. This sucked.

I looked around my father's living room. I knew everyone was sitting down except for one guy. I started feeling hate towards this man. What was he doing here? He started the intervention by introducing himself as "Tony." He said we were all gathered here to get me help.

Each person in the room read a letter to me. This was excruciatingly painful. I honestly did not want to hear what these people had to say, especially the people who were not directly involved in my life. When everyone was done reading their letters, Tony said he had a letter from my older cousin that he would read. Apparently, she had gone back to the East Coast while I was in the mental unit that she tricked me into going to.

"Stop, I've had enough. Do NOT read that letter." I said firmly. He respected my boundary.

"Now Mallory, since you have heard from your family and friends, we just want to offer you the opportunity to get help. There is a spot for you at a rehab called Harmony Haven Recovery. They have yoga and horses there and will help you get sober. Will you go?"

I felt an immense amount of pressure to say yes. My immediate family, aunt, and one family friend were all staring at me, expecting me to do the right thing. My parents had taken my phone and ID at this point, so I could not catch a flight back to Washington without my ID. I pretty much had no choice. A part of me always wanted to get sober, though. I had struggled with substance abuse since high school. This was a good chance to finally sober up.

I responded, "Yeah, I will go."

A wave of relief went around the room. Tony, the interventionist, looked especially relieved, as if I just made his job 10 times easier.

"That is so wonderful, Mallory. Ok go ahead and say bye to everyone. I will take you to Harmony Haven Recovery now."

"Ok, I need to pack a bag though!" I said.

"Mom and I already did that for you Mal," my little brother said. Wow, they really planned this whole thing out.

I walked out after saying goodbye to everyone in my family. I don't remember what type of car Tony drove, but it was small and fast. I liked it. I got in the car, and together, we drove off to Tucson from Phoenix.

This would be the last time I felt happiness and joy for a while. Tony, a middle-aged, tall white man wearing a button-down shirt, jeans, and cowboy boots, was great company on the ride there. The hate I initially felt towards him melted away once we started chatting. He clearly knew I was psychotic and made jokes with me that were almost playing into my psychosis.

"Did you know all of these signs on the road *mean* something?" he asked me. "Oh my gosh, yes I know!" I exclaimed. Finally, someone who understood.

"Everything you see around you could mean something to your life," Tony half-joked with me, feeding into my delusions. I loved Tony for this, even after getting sober. He really was able to get on my level and make me happy despite all of the trauma and quite literally losing my mind. Tony understood what I was going through, and not only put a smile on my face but helped me forget during that whole ride the pain I was feeling underneath it all.

We entered a toll road, and a camera flashed as we passed by.

He fed into my delusions once again. "Big brother is always watching," he said. This reminded me the FBI had been spying on me a few days earlier. When I looked at my Wi-Fi connection while on my laptop at my mom's house, it said "FBI", and it really freaked me out.

We stopped at a gas station to get gas and use the restroom. I got out of the car, and I could tell Tony was keeping a close eye on me. I knew it was his job to get me to that rehab.

"Is it ok if I go to the bathroom by myself? I won't run away." I asked.

"Yes, of course, I know you won't. Although I have had to chase clients who tried to get away at a gas station before." Tony chuckled under his breath.

I went to the restroom and got back into his car. We arrived at the treatment center after about two hours of driving.

# PART 2

## Chapter 1

When we pulled up to Harmony Haven Recovery, I saw it was a large ranch-like piece of property with multiple driveways. On either side of the asphalt road, there were horses grazing, a barn and small house on the right side of the road, and a large house at the top of the road.

Tony pulled up to the small house and parked. We both got out and walked inside. A woman greeted me, sat me down, and held my intake session. She asked me a million questions about myself. Tony waited in the small living area while I told this lady my life story. When I got out, he drove me further up the driveway to the large house at the top.

We both got out and this is where we said our goodbyes.

"I am leaving you here now, and I cannot hang around. I need to head out. I will be back to come check on you, though alright Mallory?" Tony said with so much kindness and compassion in his voice. He was so incredibly genuine I could not really believe it. This man had just met me, yet the empathy he showed me was beyond normal levels of human compassion. I did not want to leave him. Our car ride here was such a blast. However, I accepted it was time for him to go.

"Ok, Bye Tony. I'll see you soon." I said back to him.

I got my suitcase out of the back of his car and walked up to the house where I would be spending a good amount of time.

"Hi, my name is Rachel! I am the lead tech here and will help you finish out your intake," a lady who weighed about 250 pounds with long red hair and missing teeth greeted me. She obviously worked at this house. She led me into the "tech office", which appeared to me more like a glorious coat closet that barely had room for 1 desk and 1 chair. Rachel pulled out a pile of paperwork.

"I already did my intake down at that small house," I told Rachel.

"Yes, this is the second part. It should go much quicker; you just have to sign some paperwork."

"Ok," I replied with a bit of hesitancy in my voice.

"Here is a form saying you agree to be here for 90 days," Rachel shared as she put it down in front of me to sign.

"90 days WHAT?!" I yelled. I thought I would only be here for 30 days when I agreed to go to rehab.

"No, there must be a mistake. I am here for 30 days." I challenged Rachel.

"No, Mallory, you are here for 90 days. You need to sign here." Rachel firmly replied.

This is when it began to sink in that I was really in rehab. I did not want to be here for 90 days. Thirty days, in my mind, was more than enough. But it started to sink in that I was stranded there. No car, no phone, no ID. I had no choice but to sign. I was very reluctant and pissed off doing it though. Resentment and anger started breeding in my body. I signed the rest of the paperwork and left that "tech office."

There were two long halls full of bedrooms in the house. I was led to my room at the very end of the hall on the left from the entrance. There was a bunk bed and a full-sized bed in the room. A different tech dressed in a flannel, jeans, with long dark hair asked me to open up my suitcase. She had to inventory every single item I had brought with me and search my suitcase. I refused to open my suitcase at first. That stubborn, angsty side of me began to surface. If I did not open the suitcase, maybe I would not have to admit that I was truly here to stay. Tears welled up in my eyes. The tech was very patient with me, surprisingly. She let me stand there crying for a while before I gave in and finally opened it up.

After the tech searched my bags, I unpacked, claimed the top bunk bed and walked out of my room to the front of the house. Suddenly, a very short lady with chestnut-colored hair and a round face yelled, "Line up! It's dinner time!" I was apparently already in line, and women started pouring out of the hallway to the front of the house. There had to be at least 20 of us at the front.

The chestnut-colored hair lady, Maggy, briefly introduced herself to me and told me we were all headed to the main house for dinner. We walked together down the other side of the asphalt driveway and stopped at the front of the main house. Together, we all got into a circle, bowed our heads, and prayed. At the end of the prayer, all of the women put one of their feet in the middle of the circle and shouted, "Stay!" This all felt strangely cult-like but the prayer did calm my spirit a bit.

We lined up inside the main house to get food. My hands started shaking. I was so anxious. Everything was happening so quickly in a whirlwind-like fashion. Intervention…boom…drive with Tony…boom…intake…boom…unpack…boom….20 women around me…boom…dinner time…boom.

When I got to the front of the line, I saw the cook who made our dinner standing behind the buffet. He was giving me a strange look. He must have known I was the new girl. This made me even shakier and more anxious. I put salad, chicken, and potatoes on my plate. I made a slight twist to the left, lost control of my plate, and BAM, it fell and shattered all over the floor. I immediately burst into tears, making the situation feel even worse.

About 5 women immediately started cleaning up the mess, and one lady named Ashley, with green eyes and long blonde hair, started consoling me.

"It's ok. I know it is crazy ending up in rehab. This must have been a very difficult day for you. Go sit down. We will clean this food and broken plate up, and I will make you a new plate with food."

By the time we finished dinner, it started pouring rain outside. Water was pounding on the floor. One of the techs from the women's house drove a van up to the main house to pick us up so we did not have to walk back in the pouring rain.

We all ran outside quickly, and the front three-quarters of the group piled in the van. They all sat in the front so it was very difficult for the last of us to arrange ourselves and fit. I waited in the pouring rain, getting drenched as the women in the van tried to make space for the rest of us.

The rain made the entire day that much more surreal.

We eventually made it back to the women's house. Bed time rolled around, and I tried to settle into my new quarters. It seemed like everyone in the house fell asleep so quickly. It was quiet right away. I tossed and turned in bed until, eventually, I could not take it any longer. I climbed out of my top bunk and walked into the living room.

I curled up on the couch with no blanket and started talking to God. I was upset with him. I told him - I am scared, God, I am here, and I do not know a soul. Why am I here while my family is comfortable at home? Why am I the one in rehab? I am angry, God, I am angry.

The night tech came out of her office and asked me what I was doing. I told her this was my first night here, and I could not sleep.

She gave me a brief, empathetic look, then told me I needed to go back to bed. With no other choice, back to bed, I went.

Over the next couple of weeks, I slowly started getting adjusted to being in rehab. The first time I met with my counselor for a session, Cheryl, I was so pissed off I couldn't stop yelling and screaming at her. I told her angrily that it was not fair that I was the one in rehab while my family was happy at home. She did not try to stop me from yelling. She let me scream in her face and sat there silently. Although it was completely unfair she was getting the brunt of my anger, her compassion was so great and she was so kind that she let me process my emotions the only way at that time I knew how - by screaming. When I was done expressing myself, I stormed out of her office, which was in the women's house, slammed the door and went outside to sit on the front porch swing.

There was absolutely nothing I could do to make myself feel better. I just had to sit there and stew in my anger. Anytime, before rehab, I could drink or smoke to calm myself down. But not here. I started crying on the porch swing.

"Mallory." I heard a voice behind me. I turned around quickly and saw Tony standing on the porch. Where did he come from? I did not hear him walk or drive up. He had a glow around his entire body. He looked like an angel to me.

"Are you ok?" he asked.

"No, I am SO angry," I shared.

Tony had a healing presence - just standing there with me helped calm me down. The look on his face was so deeply empathetic. Just the way he held himself, I could tell he knew exactly what I was going through.

"I'm so sorry, Mallory. But let me explain. The feelings inside of you are all knotted up like a big ball of tangled yarn. This is all of the pain, trauma, and fear inside of you. While you are here at Harmony Haven Recovery, you will slowly begin to pull strings out of this knot. At first, it will be difficult, but when you get more momentum, the entire ball of yarn will slowly become united again. Do you understand?"

I nodded my head. I loved Tony. He was so sweet.

"Here!" He handed me a toothbrush and some toothpaste. "Your counselor told me you needed this."

I was so grateful I needed a real toothpaste and toothbrush. The one my mom and brother packed was a tiny little toothbrush, and they did not pack toothpaste either.

"Thank you so much, Tony; I needed this," I said.

"You're welcome. Well, I just came here to see you and drop this off. I'll come check on you again later. Take care." Tony gave me a big hug, jumped back into his speedy little car parked in front of the women's house, and took off.

# Chapter 2

I quickly got into the routine set out for me and the 20 other ladies in treatment. The schedule below was a typical day at Harmony Haven Recovery.

Wake Up

Meditate for 30 minutes

 Breakfast

Group therapy

Work Out

Free Time

Lunch

More group therapy

Work on the 12 steps

Free Time

Dinner

12 Step meeting

Night time review

Bed time

We each had individual therapy and equine therapy once a week, sometimes during programming as well.

This was the most structure I ever had in my entire life, and I was there for 3 whole months. It was like an emotional boot camp. The daily meditation practice was incredibly healing for my nervous system. I was so dysregulated coming into treatment, suffering from rapid cycling mania and depression. Every day, someone would read scripture and the 11-step passage from the big book. But taking 30 minutes every morning to contemplate the readings, breathe, and center myself for the day ahead was actually quite revolutionary. There were things I hated about rehab (like having to do 20 women's dishes after meals, sharing a room with other angry recovering addicts, scooping horse poop in equine therapy, doing "team building exercises," sharing with the women how I felt during accountability group) but meditation was my absolute favorite part of the day. I would pour myself a large cup of coffee at 6:27 AM and be seated in the living room for meditation right at 6:30 AM on the dot.

I grew very close to my counselor, Cheryl as I met with her every week. When I saw her for the second time, I wasn't so full of rage, and I apologized for screaming at her. She told me that she understood and I didn't have to apologize. Cheryl helped me understand why I felt like my family members let me down growing up. My expectations for them were too high, and when they could not meet my expectations, I was disappointed. I learned that no one else on this planet will ever be able to fully meet my expectations. This helped me realize why building a relationship with God is so important. I can't rely on other people to meet my expectations, but I can lean on a higher power to make me feel safe.

I grappled with my spirituality the entire time I was in rehab. In Washington and Oregon, I had multiple hallucinations and incredibly powerful out-of-body experiences. Communicating with aliens in Portland left a huge impression on me. This was a product of my drug-induced and mania-induced psychosis. Psychosis is a state of mind where the individual experiencing it is not in reality. They often cannot accomplish simple everyday tasks such as taking care of themselves or going to work when they are not in touch with reality. Individuals experiencing psychosis can have delusions, paranoia, hallucinations, trouble thinking clearly or logically, and also tend to isolate themselves.

At night, in treatment, I would go on the back porch and look up at the Milky Way. Harmony Haven Recovery was located outside of the city, so the night sky was incredible. I would stare at the sky for an hour or so, looking for UFOs almost every night. Some of the other women were concerned about me because of how obsessed I was with aliens and the stars. Clearly, I was still processing my psychosis. But I did have one friend who would help me look for UFOs.

During my free time I would spend time staring at myself in the mirror, and I didn't recognize the person looking back at me. Mallory, my old self, was gone. My hair was chopped off, and my eyes looked dark and empty. My face was hollow and too thin. I did not know who I was and struggled to know who God was, too.

As days progressed in treatment, I worked the 12 steps of Alcoholics Anonymous. Steps 1-3 were relatively easy. The fourth step took hours and days to complete. I had to write down all of my resentments, the fears associated with them, how these fears affected me, and also write down my part in these resentments. I wrote 90 pages about my resentments and how they affected me. I was so incredibly resentful, and I didn't even know it. The writing came out like word vomit. It's almost like I was past the point of being ready to get all of this nasty emotional poison out on paper.

I am a writer, always have been, and always will be. And this writing exercise is what freed my soul. I would grab a blanket and hide in the corner of Harmony Haven Recovery property outside while working on my fourth step. I would lie down with my blanket under me, write for hours at a time, and sneak puffs off my vape. Vaping while working on 12-step work was not allowed, but I did it anyway. My rebellious side came out again, even while doing step work.

After finishing up my 4th step, it was time to move on to the 5th step, which is "Admitted to God, to ourselves, and to another human being the exact nature of our wrongs." In order to do this I had to sit down with someone and read every single page I had written and share all of my resentments and fears.

Maggy volunteered to listen to my 5th step, which, in my eyes, was awfully generous of her. We walked outside to the bench in the backyard of the house while the rest of the women were in an AA meeting inside. It was fairly late, 6 in the evening. We brought flash lights to continue the process after the sun went down. I genuinely thanked Maggy for listening to all of this. She laughed sweetly and said, "Of course, Mallory. It's not like I have anywhere else to be." We both thought that was pretty funny.

I shared with her my resentments against each member of my family except my younger brother. I did not have one resentment against him. I went on to talk about my resentments with the friends I partied with. I shared resentments against past teachers and friends from elementary school, middle school, high school, and college. I shared the resentment I had against my old coach. I shared many resentments that night.

The sun went down as I processed and admitted these resentments and fears. I took my flash light out and used it to read off resentment after resentment. Moths were attracted to the light and I could hear crickets making loud noises in the desert that surrounded us. It took me a total of three hours to share all 90 pages with Maggy. At the very end, we prayed to God to wrap things up, and very suddenly, I felt a very intense yet beautiful energy envelop me. I felt a heaviness on my shoulders completely leave my body. This beautiful energy made my heart whole and brought deep peace to my entire soul. The healing I felt was so incredibly intense, and I wanted this moment to last forever. This was a burning bush spiritual experience in sobriety.

There is no other way to explain it. Looking back and reflecting on this spiritual experience, I know it was the Holy Spirit returning my soul to my body and sending the darkness inside of me away. Unfortunately, the moment did have to end as we wrapped up the prayer, but I was so incredibly confident God's presence was all around me when we finished.

It is traditional in the AA program to meditate for one hour after completing a 5th step. The rest of the women were all in bed, but I was allowed to stay up and meditate to process everything that just happened. I sat down cross-legged on the floor, placed my hands on my knees, and shut my eyes. My mind was completely still, and I was at peace for the first time in years. As I sat there with my eyes closed, I saw Jesus appear to me behind my eyelids. He gazed deeply at me, acknowledged me, and then he swooped down into my heart and disappeared behind my eyelids. I am not sure how long I had meditated for, but I knew a visit from Jesus was all I needed to complete the night. I slowly stood up and went off to bed, knowing I was comforted and blessed that night.

# Chapter 3

The next couple of days, I felt light as a feather. Releasing all of those resentment and fears changed who I was to the very core. The second night after my fifth step I laid down in my bunk to fall asleep. After about 45 minutes, I felt the sharpest pain in my stomach that I had ever felt in my life. I immediately jumped off my bunk and ran to the restroom. I violently vomited into the toilet. I purged about five times. This was yet another powerful experience that followed my 5th step. This was not just a normal "throw up." I had felt something leave my body that night while I purged. I am not sure what left - it could have been energy, deep-seated pain, more darkness, or even a demon or entity. But after I was done purging, I was absolutely exhausted. I cleaned up the puke that got everywhere on the toilet from the violent projectile and immediately went to bed.

The next morning, I slept in. My body was spent from puking the night before. It was definitely frowned upon to sleep in while in treatment. Harmony Haven Recovery was strict about getting out of bed on time for meditation. The night tech must have reported that I got violently ill because they did not even try to push me out of bed that morning when I told Rachel, the day tech, that I physically could not get out of bed.

I slept in until mid-morning and got up to join the rest of the programming. I did not think I could feel this free in my entire life. Not only did I feel light as a feather, but I also felt completely surrendered to this process. Some of the women shared with me that they heard me puking from all the way down the hall. Ashley said that it is a good thing to purge after doing spiritual work because it cleanses the body and soul. I asked the women if anyone else got sick last night. I thought perhaps it could have been food poisoning from the dinner the night before. Not one single other lady got sick. I was convinced this was another intense spiritual experience. I was absolutely amazed by the Holy Spirit visit after my fifth step, Jesus coming to me while I meditated and then purging out what I believed to be the demon of addiction. These experiences proved to me that I do not need to use substances to be spiritual. God can work in my life and give me powerful experiences without them. What an amazing journey he had brought me on, and I wasn't even done with my treatment yet!

After my fifth step experiences the rest of my treatment went by very quickly. The first half was extremely painful and difficult to get through. As I felt so lost, afraid, and empty inside. After my fifth step I was full of life. Instead of dragging through each day, I surrendered. I participated fully. There were still many challenges I had to face, don't get me wrong, but I had life inside of me to keep me going.

I was still suffering from mania and psychosis. During group therapy, a woman shared a very sad story about someone close to her dying, and I was so manic at the time I burst out laughing and could not stop. I felt so embarrassed and ashamed that I was laughing, but I could not control my emotions. I left that group therapy session and went outside to try and figure out what was going on with myself. I was having a manic outburst.

My mom told me she spoke with my counselor while I was in treatment on several occasions. My mom shared that although I had been struggling with substance abuse, she knew I probably had some other mental health issues as well underneath the substance use disorder. My mom wanted me to be evaluated by a psychiatrist, but my counselor shared that I needed to be sober for at least a year in order for a psychiatrist to figure out what was really going on with me beneath the substance use. This made my mom angry, she wanted me to get evaluated sooner. But she did not want to take me out of the treatment program.

The rest of the time I spent in treatment passed, and I was feeling even better towards the end. Exercising in the gym three times a week contributed to my well-being.

I was in incredible shape by the end of the three months physically. My second to last day of treatment rolled around and it was time for my send off ceremony. This is when all 20 women in treatment would circle up with the counselors and pass a coin around, wishing the person leaving inpatient good luck and saying encouraging words, charging the coin. I remember feeling a bit anxious while everyone addressed me in the closing circle.

One counselor told me that I had a very moldable mind, I am very teachable, and that I pick up on new ideas quickly. She gave me a warning to not let my mind be too open. I appreciated that warning as I had always been extremely curious and open to a fault. My counselor, Cheryl, shared that I was the ideal Harmony Haven client and that I worked very hard on improving myself emotionally and spiritually. She shared that I had made incredible progress during my three months at inpatient and she was so very proud of me. This made me feel warm inside and grateful to have her blessing as I was getting ready to leave.

After we closed out the circle, I sprinted back to my room at the end of the hall and just burst into tears. I felt like I had just been through an incredibly intense whirlwind and that I had been through the wringer. Not only did I have multiple spiritual burning bush experiences, but I also lived with 20 women for 3 months, spent very long hours examining my internal landscape, and changed so many things about myself with God's help. It was a good change, though. I did not feel defeated, but I was in absolute awe of what God had done for me that I couldn't do myself - get sober and experience a whole new dimension of internal freedom.

That night I packed up my things, binders of worksheets and information the counselors gave me, written step work, and even some clothes my mom sent to me in a package.

The next morning, I ate breakfast with the women one last time and waited in the living room for my ride. A few weeks before my discharge, my counselor encouraged me to continue treatment and go to Harmony Haven Sober Living Women's House in Tucson.

Through the process of being in rehab, I fully surrendered to the program and accepted further help after inpatient rehab.

Tony showed up for my last day to send me off and wish me well for the next step in my journey. "Tony!!!" I yelled when he showed up. He had surprised me. "What are you doing here?"

"I'm sending you off, Mallory! I am so incredibly proud of you and all of the work you have done. I know what you went through over these past 3 months was not easy. You did it!"

"Aww, thank you so much, Tony!" I gave him a big hug. That's when Cheryl walked out of her office.

"Cheryl was your mama while you were here! Give her a big hug, too!"

I turned to give Cheryl a big hug. "Thank you so much for everything, Cheryl! I will miss you so much at sober living."

"I am so incredibly proud of you, Mallory," Cheryl told me again.

Cheryl and Tony were my angels during that time in my life, and I will be forever grateful to both of them.

I loaded my suitcase into the back of the car that would be taking me to Harmony Haven Sober Living. A tech drove me from Harmony Haven Recovery inpatient to their sober living.

We arrived at the house, and I unloaded my stuff and hauled it up the 5 stairs leading to the front porch of the house. The house manager greeted me and asked me to fill out some paperwork. By this point, I was used to filling out forms when transferring to a new location. She also went through my stuff, which I did not have much of, and showed me where I would be sleeping upstairs.

My room had a bunk bed and, two standard twin-sized beds and a beautiful master bathroom with a huge tub. I was happy to see that the top bunk was open. I unpacked my clothes, hung them in the closet, and stored my suitcase in the garage. I would be here for three more months in addition to the three months of inpatient, on top of the hospital stay I had in Phoenix.

I knew most of the women in the Harmony Haven Sober Living house because they had been in rehab with me at the Harmony Haven Recovery inpatient facility. There were a couple of other women I did not recognize but they were so very friendly and introduced themselves to me when I arrived.

The main house had three bedrooms, a living room, an office, a large kitchen, and a very cozy den at the front. There was also a back house across the backyard with two bedrooms, a living room, and a kitchenette, all on the second floor. The garage was under the back house on the first floor.

There was a three-level tier system to graduate from Harmony Haven Sober Living. Only the women on level 3 were allowed to stay in the back house. They had completed intensive outpatient and found jobs.

Maggy, the woman who listened to my fifth step, was there! It was so good to see her again. She had graduated from inpatient six weeks before me.

"Mallory, it's so good to see you!" Maggy greeted me. "Want me to tell you more about Harmony Haven Sober Living?"

"Maggy, hey! You look great! Yes, a run-down would be perfect," I replied.

"OK, so we cook in the kitchen every night for dinner. We cook in pairs and rotate every night who cooks dinner. Every week, we write down what we want for groceries for the week, and the staff gets them and delivers them for us. For the first two months, you will be in intensive outpatient programming, also known as IOP. In IOP, you see a counselor once a week and participate in groups. It is very similar to programming at inpatient, except it is only three hours a day instead of all day long! We work out and do CrossFit three times a week and yoga at the house once a week. Every morning, we do our daily assigned chores, and every Sunday, we deep clean the entire house for three to five hours. We go to an AA meeting every night. We are also required to work on the steps with a sponsor again while we are here. Any questions so far?"

"Yes! I heard we get our phones at Harmony Haven Sober Living! How often do we get to use them?"

"Haha, great question!" Maggy replied, "We get to use our phones in the morning and in the evening after programming, but other than that, our phone time is limited. The techs here are pretty strict on phone use. And we are not allowed to take our phones to the bedrooms, we can only use them downstairs. Oh, and one more thing: we can only text. We are not allowed to call anyone or FaceTime anyone. If you want to make a phone call, you need to request to use the house phone."

I thanked Maggy for giving me the rundown of Harmony Haven Sober Living and immediately walked to the office to request my phone. I had been praying for Derrick every single night for the past three months in rehab, and I wanted to check in on him as soon as possible. I had so many questions to ask him. Did he end up getting help? Where was he in the United States? Was he sober? Was he sane? Did he still care about me? Did he want to be with me? Did he love me? Did he remember everything that happened in Washington?

I asked the house manager, Amy, if she had my phone and if I could use it.

"You have to settle in for a couple of days before you get your phone," she stated with a matter-of-fact, slightly forceful tone.

Ugh, this was so annoying. I responded respectfully that I understood, but on the inside, I was frustrated. It was difficult having all of my privileges taken away from me. I was frustrated that this woman had control over what I could and could not do. But I let it go and joined some ladies in the living room to chill.

One thing I quickly learned was that we were allowed to take walks or go for runs in the quaint neighborhood of the Harmony Haven Sober Living property. I took advantage of this privilege immediately because being in a house with 18 other women at a time was full of drama.

Especially women who were newly sober and still figuring out how to "do" life without using substances. I was in the exact same boat, but I did try my absolute best to stay out of unnecessary fights and conflict. The house at inpatient was probably three times the size of the Harmony Haven Sober Living house. There was much more space to hide and escape from all of the crazy hormones and people detoxing at inpatient. At Harmony Haven Sober Living, not so much.

# Chapter 4

After a couple of days of settling in, I finally got my phone. My father had bought me a brand new iPhone 7, and had his secretary send it to Harmony Haven Sober Living so it was waiting for me when I arrived. I was so excited; I thought it was so incredibly kind of him. I was not expecting a new phone, and when the house manager gave me the sleek brand new iPhone in the Apple box wrapped in plastic, I could not wait to open it and activate it.

It was gold and beautiful. The moment I turned it on, I felt a new kind of freedom wash over me. Call me ridiculous, but I was a millennial who had gone without the internet or a cell phone for over three whole months at that point. This was for sure the longest I had ever gone without the internet up to this point in my life.

When my phone activated, a whole flood of text messages pinged my phone, and Facebook messages came flooding in, too when I downloaded the Facebook Messenger app. It gave me a big dopamine rush. People were checking in on me, asking me if I was ok, and asking where I was. I immediately downloaded my contacts from the cloud and texted Derrick. No response for a while. I knew from talking to other women and friends in meetings it was very common for people to get a new phone number when they get sober to eliminate contact with old drug dealers and friends who used. I had a hunch that maybe Derrick ended up in rehab and got a new number.

I messaged his best friend on Facebook and asked him if he had Derrick's number. BINGO! He replied right away, telling me he did, in fact, have a new number. He immediately sent Derrick's new contact info. This was all very exciting - Derrick felt like a world away while I was in rehab, but now I was about to actually make contact with him. And no, not alien contact, but real human contact through a phone!

I texted him, and he responded about half an hour later after getting out of his yoga class. It turns out when he was discharged from the psych hospital in Washington, he was immediately transferred to a treatment facility in New Mexico. But by the time he arrived, he was extremely overmedicated and could barely function. He refused to go to programming, which was unacceptable to this facility, so they helped him find a better fit for him at a treatment center based in California. That's when a psychiatrist helped him adjust his medications, and eventually, he was able to participate in the program.

When we texted each other we communicated like rapid fire. I was so thrilled to find out he was working towards his sobriety and had been over the past three months, just like me. I thought we had a good chance of working things out since we were both on the same page. We were working on our mental health and staying clean. I prayed for Derrick every single night while I was in rehab.

God had answered my prayers and took care of him while we were separated, and the good Lord was now giving our relationship another shot.

As I began the three-month Harmony Haven Sober Living program, I had a good attitude and hope in my heart. We got to spend time on our phones in the morning before programming and in the evening afterwards. Every chance I got, I was texting Derrick. I even used the house phone to call him a few times, but we texted on a regular basis.

My meditation practice continued while I was in Harmony Haven Sober Living. We meditated on readings as a house first thing in the morning. But I would also spend time meditating on my top bunk during free time as well. Sydney, a good friend of mine who was also in Harmony Sober Living treatment, lent me a book to enhance my clairvoyant abilities. I spent a couple of hours a week flipping through the pages and practicing the exercises. I also bought a book at the half price book shop about chakras. It had information about kundalini awakenings. I read that if they happen in an unregulated environment, the energy can burst through the crown chakra, and it can cause psychosis. The kundalini awakening made my psychosis worse. I knew this was what happened to me.

During my stay at inpatient, I would try to leave my body regularly to astral project. This is a New Age practice where the individual falls into a deep meditative state, calms their body to the point it is almost asleep, and wills the soul to disconnect from the body using their mind to fly on the astral plane. When I was in Washington, I dissociated to the point that my soul was flying through space. I wanted nothing more than to go back there. I just did not want to have to deal with the traumatic part of coming back down to my body.

I never successfully left my body while at inpatient, but God did bless me with a very vivid spiritual experience while I was in Harmony Haven Sober Living.

One afternoon after intensive outpatient programming, I laid down on my top bunk in the room alone, staring at photos in the clairvoyant book meant to induce meditative states. I stared at a photo of a blue flower and gently laid down to try and leave my body. I fell asleep, and the next thing I knew, I was lucid dreaming. I was standing in a gorgeous glowing gold field, and Our Lady of Guadalupe appeared to me in the sky. She was in the clouds wearing bright clothing, and I immediately knew it was her. A beautiful vibration flowed through my body, and the Holy Spirit washed over me.

Mother Mary told me, "You now have access to the spirit world; use this privilege wisely and for good, not evil."

And then she left just as quickly as she appeared. In my dream, I laid down in the field and started believing I could fly. I left my body and started soaring towards the sunset. It was absolutely incredible - I was completely free. The sun was burning brightly - my soul was attracted to it like a magnet. As I was flying across the field toward the sun, something inside of me told me to turn around, and I caught a glimpse of two men with dark hair standing on a cliff. I flew past them back to the golden field where my body was lying down.

From this point, I felt a little fear and then heard someone say, "You are now in the spirit world; you may begin."

Still in the dream I decided to return back to my body. Then, I woke up on my bunk at Harmony Haven Sober Living. I prayed to Mary and thanked her, then went on a walk with a few of the women in the house.

That evening, the memories of my lucid dream came flooding back to me, and I thought about the two men that I saw on the cliff. All of a sudden, I realized it was my uncle standing with one of his friends. I texted my uncle and asked him if he had watched the sunset on a cliff today. When I saw his response, chills washed over my body, and I started to sweat. My uncle texted back, "Yes, I watched the sunset off of a bluff." It was a miracle.

I texted back, 'I was there in spirit :)' To me, this was undeniable proof that everything I experienced in my lucid dream was real - Mary appearing, me leaving my body, and soaring towards the sun. I knew in my heart that it was real, but this was just extra confirmation

That night, I asked the women in the sober living house if we could watch the movie 'Inception' with Leonardo DiCaprio. In this movie, the main character dives deep into the subconscious - going from a dream within a dream within a dream.

Day after day, I showed up at IOP and fulfilled my duties as a member of the house. But I was far from stable; I was hypomanic and still suffering from psychosis. I was living with bipolar type 1, unmedicated, and raw-dogging sobriety. On top of it all - I was bursting with energy every single day. One woman in the house would joke around with me, completely unaware I was hypomanic, and say, "Give me a hug so I can get some of that energy, girl!"

My engines were running full throttle day in and day out, but I was still able to sleep at night. That was my saving grace, and I believe it spared me from being hospitalized a second time. I was extremely goal-oriented. I worked the steps diligently with my sponsor, participated in groups, cleaned the house every day, and texted Derrick on a regular basis. But when I was under the spell of psychosis, I would research twin flames, the healing properties of crystals, yogis leaving their bodies, chakras, and astral projection, pouring over as much as I could on my laptop.

During group sessions with the women at the house, we would bring up "concerns" that we'd notice about each other - issues that might interfere with our sobriety. One woman at the house gave me a "concern" during a group that I was too obsessed with researching New Age beliefs and that I was not grounding appropriately like I needed to. Another woman gave me a "concern" that I was too focused on texting Derrick rather than being present in the household. It was hard to admit to myself, but they were right. I broke up with Derrick after giving it some thought. I told him I needed a break from the relationship while I finished out my treatment.

I did not let up, however, on researching New Age spirituality. I was completely obsessed. It was my new escape from reality, fueling my psychotic mindset. I started diving into astrology and how it affected my 'twin flame journey' with Derrick. I read many, many blog posts on twin flames. This is a New Age concept that one soul can be split into two parts and those two soul parts incarnate in two bodies. Both souls then go on a journey to be reunited on Earth. At one point, I found out about the world of twin flame cults. Leaders were charging members thousands of dollars for "twin flame coaching." Cult members were so desperate to find the other halves that they forked over A LOT of money for help. But it was eventually clear to me that these leaders just wanted their money and brainwashed them by ruining their self-esteem.

I paid $10 for a twin flame meditation but, luckily, was not sucked into an online twin flame cult. I read about the chakras, the stars, angel numbers, spirit animals, omens, and more. All of these teachings were confusing and contradictory at times, but I was obsessed with and addicted to magical thinking. I was still lost and under the influence of Satan.

# Chapter 5

In my last month of treatment, I got a job as a front desk coordinator at a spa resort in Tucson. It was a requirement to start working before I could graduate and I really enjoyed every minute. The grounds were covered with native plants, and there was a pond at the bottom of a hill that felt very peaceful. This was a 5-star resort, and for the most part, the guests were pleasant. It was my first introduction to working in an industry that focused on healing. I got to know all of the massage therapists and estheticians. They had a healing presence, and I enjoyed chit-chatting with them as I prepared products for their clients.

Another perk - I got a free treatment once a month to get to know the spa menu better, and I was allowed to use the pool after getting off work. The spa director would even let me use the hot tub and steam room after work occasionally.

After taking some time apart, Derrick and I started communicating again on my last day at Harmony Haven Sober Living. On Valentine's Day, I called him to tell him that I was leaving the house and ready to let him in again. He was so kind and loving that day. Even though I broke his heart, he still waited for me and understood the pressure I was getting from the other women to "focus on myself."

Leaving this sober living was not as intense as graduating from inpatient. All of the women sat in a circle and said nice things to me while holding a small crystal. In the end, after everyone took their turn, the house manager handed me the "charged" crystal and wished me good luck.

A day earlier, my dad and sister-in-law drove my Subaru all the way from Phoenix to Tucson and dropped it off at sober living. It was waiting for me in the driveway the day I left. It felt so good to throw my stuff into the car and drive off. When I first entered inpatient, my dad flew up to Washington again. He packed up my entire apartment - picking up the pieces of my broken life while I got some serious help.

I don't take for granted what he did for me. It took a lot of energy and effort on his part. When I made amends to my father as a part of my step work, I thanked him sincerely for everything he did.

I had graduated from Harmony Haven Sober Living, but I still had a long way to go before living on my own. I then went to another sober living house. My new home, for now, was a bridge to the real world. I had gotten closer and closer to stepping back in without the guardrails, but the goal was to get me back into society and be able to handle it sober.

The requirements to live here were I had to stay sober, I had to go to a 12-step meeting every single day, and I had to do chores. Other than that, there was a lot more freedom in this house.

I picked up more hours at the spa - working seven-hour shifts, five days a week. Derrick and I talked on the phone every day, which helped motivate me to keep up my routine and sobriety. As long as I was doing what I needed to be doing, I was that much closer to visiting Derrick. It was Valentine's Day when I moved, and we decided I would fly to Los Angeles to visit him by mid-March.

But by this point, there was a shift. My boundless energy started fading, and darkness started creeping in. I was so happy with how far I had come and the fact that I was holding down a job, but when I laid down in bed at night, the depression would take hold. Some nights, I even had thoughts of killing myself. Suicidal thoughts became my norm. Fortunately, work kept me busy, so I only had time to be suicidal at night. But on my days off, when I had time to sink deep into my thoughts, it was much harder to keep the sick, dark feelings at bay. It was maddening because, by all accounts, things were finally going well for me. So why did I feel this way? Some days, I would lie down outside on the concrete driveway in hopes that the sun's rays would improve my mood. But nothing seemed to work; I still felt so incredibly depressed, with a heaviness weighing down on my soul.

I learned the hard way that after years of being undiagnosed with a mental health condition, I had no firm anchor or baseline for my mood. Hypomania and depression were my norms; I just didn't realize it. It was all I knew. And that's a problem that many people struggle with. Until they get diagnosed by a medical professional, they think that their erratic thoughts, depression, inattention, or lack of impulse control will always be in the background. Those around you, especially people who are close to you, might not understand what you are going through because they are used to the ups and downs and erratic mood cycles. Also, if they have never been exposed to someone who has mental health problems and they're not educated on mental health as well, they can be clueless as to what is actually going on.

At this point, my depression and suicidal thoughts were still manageable to an extent because I was still able to wake up and face the day every morning. But nightly reflections and therapy helped me confront the feelings that threatened to consume me. The pendulum of my illness was swinging in the opposite direction, and I needed to pull myself out without falling back the other way - like I was at Harmony Haven Sober Living. But my job and the anticipation of seeing Derrick again helped stop me from giving up.

A month passed, and it was time for me to go see Derrick in Los Angeles. Excitement pulsed through my veins as I got dressed for the airport. I wore a long blue skirt, a grey tank top with a feathered dream catcher on it, and a tan colored fedora. The flight was relaxing and relatively quick. I immediately whipped my phone out and texted Derrick when we touched down, and I couldn't get off the plane fast enough. During some of the most painful moments of rehab, I was afraid I might never see or touch Derrick again, but there he was, walking towards me in the baggage claim. We grabbed each other and held one another so incredibly tight. We both took a few deep breaths while clinging to each other, then let go. Then we kissed each other many times while tears welled up in my eyes. We then paused for a moment, looking at each other. I thought to myself, *I can't believe after everything, we are here together.*

Derrick helped me get my luggage, and he drove me to his parent's house, where he was living. We had the loveliest time being reunited after 9 months of being apart. Every time I looked at him, electricity shot through my body and I felt ecstatic when we were physical with each other.

Derrick drove me out to Malibu, and we spent the day on the beach. We kissed, laughed, and held each other as we lay in the sand and watched the surfers ride the waves rolling in. We stayed there until the sun went down.

One night, Derrick drove me up to the top of a valley. We sat on the top of his parents' Acura and listened to Bob Moses while holding each other close. The wind was blowing, and we could see millions of city lights shining down below us. We wore sweatpants and sweatshirts and were cozy and warm that spring night.

Derrick gazed at me while I watched the city lights twinkle below. He subtly pulled out a small box.

"Mallory, we have been through so much together, and I want to keep you in my life forever. Will you marry me?" he asked. He opened the box, and it had a gold tungsten band in it. I said yes without hesitation and slipped the gold tungsten band on my left ring finger. The moment felt right, and I was so in love. I did not expect him to ask me to marry him so quickly, but our connection was undeniable.

When I got back to Tucson, I broke the news to my family and my sober living house that I was engaged. My family did not support me, and it felt like they looked down on me. They were disappointed I got engaged to someone I hit rock bottom with. Getting engaged was supposed to be one of the happiest times of my life, but my family didn't see it that way. They all thought Derrick and I were still too unstable to make this kind of commitment. I definitely felt stigmatized for having mental illness and addiction problems. I was 9 months sober, yet it felt like no one cared or recognized all of the hard work I had put into getting well. They didn't know what it was like to be unstable or psychotic, and they thought I wasn't capable of making a decision like this myself. It was beyond frustrating.

I carried on with my life in sober living while planning a trip to Bali to become certified as a yoga teacher. Derrick found a yoga teacher training on an Indonesian island. He supported my dreams of becoming a yoga teacher. The program was an Ashtanga/Yin yoga teacher training which are two opposite kinds of yoga. While in sober living, I took twenty 90-minute Ashtanga classes to prepare my body for the intense three-week training. I would practice the Ashtanga sequence on the back porch of my sober living house in between work and meetings.

Summer rolled around, and it was time for me to fly to the other side of the world. I left my job at the spa on good terms and moved out of sober living. I drove back to my mom's house in Phoenix to pack for Bali. I could tell my mom was extremely anxious about me going to Bali to do yoga with less than a year of sobriety under my belt. But I had learned in rehab not to be as codependent with my family members - I needed to take my own path. It was not my responsibility to calm her down or make her feel better. I was going to Bali regardless. Looking back, I understand why she was so incredibly nervous to see me go off on my own. I had a track record of getting involved with cults, becoming psychotic, engaging in New Age practices and making friends with people who were also seriously mentally ill. Knowing my mom, she gave me over to God as I took off and left the United States behind.

# PART 3

## Chapter 1

I took off for Beijing, China out of the Seattle airport on a Delta Flight. About 45 minutes into the flight the pilot made an announcement over the loudspeakers.

"Ladies and gentlemen, this is the pilot speaking. We are currently turning the plane around and heading back to the Seattle Airport. There was an incident on the plane that needs to be addressed. We will be landing shortly." Everyone I saw sitting around me perked up and started looking around. We had no idea what had happened.

When we landed, I found out a man in first class had assaulted a flight attendant. All 210 passengers deboarded the flight when it landed back in Seattle. We waited in the airport for four hours and then were finally cleared to reboard the plane.

After a 10-hour flight, I landed in Beijing. I got lost in the Beijing airport and still, to this day am not quite sure how I found my gate. I could not read the signs. I did see a Starbucks in the airport, though; it was like a beacon of light that honed me in at the airport. I ordered something random off the menu. I had no idea what it said - the menu was in a Chinese language. The barista gave me a grande cup filled with coconut water and a shot of espresso. It tasted delicious. I had never seen this on the Starbucks menu in the United States. Even though I was confused and a bit lost, I felt free.

I boarded a seven-hour flight to Denpasar, a city in Bali, from Beijing after a 3-hour layover. After a 23-hour journey, when I landed in Denpasar, a short Balinese man picked me up in a van and drove me to my hostel.

I checked into my private hostel room and showered. Although exhausted, that did not stop me from exploring the streets. I took a stroll around the town to soak in the vibes of Bali. There were rows of vendors selling bright-colored pants and shirts, each of them beckoning me to check out their little shops. On every corner, there were little flowers and incense offerings. The streets smelled very nice.

I walked to a restaurant down the street from my hostel and ordered chicken and rice with an iced tea. When I was finished, I walked back to my hostel and laid down on the bed. I couldn't keep my eyes open even though the sun was still up. I slept for 14+ hours. After a year of rehab and sober living, plus traveling around the world, my soul was exhausted. When I woke up I had to orient myself, reminding myself I was in Bali. I slowly got out of bed and got my things together. My yoga teacher training was starting that evening and I had to catch a ferry to the next island over.

A jeep was waiting for me where the ferry stopped and dropped me off at the tiny hotel where I'd be staying for the next three weeks to learn how to teach yoga.

The hotel staff was welcoming, and my living quarters were surrounded by lush tropical plants and flowers. I had a master bedroom with an armoire, a bathroom, and an outdoor private shower. There was a deep blue fresh water pool just steps from my front door. There was a little hotel cafe where I could get Balinese Coffee and banana pancakes in the morning. The beach was a 5-minute walk from where I was staying, and the yoga shala where I did my training was a 10-minute walk from the little hotel.

After getting settled, I met a few other yoga students sitting in the cabanas next to me. When it was time for the opening ceremony, we all went together.

We walked to the shala, an outdoor space where we would be practicing yoga. When we got there yoga students were already introducing themselves to each other around a fresh flower mandala in the middle of the floor. The two teachers leading the training were quite opposites of each other, but their personalities matched the type of yoga that they each taught. The Ashtanga teacher was French and very serious. The Yin teacher was American and very laid back and compassionate.

After the opening ceremony, we all went to the cafe in front of the shala to eat an organic dinner. We ended up eating all three meals there unless I wanted to eat breakfast alone at the hotel. It was the freshest food I had ever eaten - the chicken was farm-raised, the fish was directly from the Indian ocean, and the juices and smoothie bowls were sweet. At the two long wooden tables is where we all got to know each other, laughed, joked around, and nourished our bodies. There were men and women from Denmark, France, New Zealand, Hungary, Spain, and the United States. We all had different accents and spoke English to communicate with each other.

Every morning, we arrived at the shala at 6 AM to start our Ashtanga yoga practice. A few times a week, it would rain and we would be doing yoga as the sun came up by the sound of pit pattering on the shala roof. The series I was trying to master, the Ashtanga Primary Series, was very challenging. Each of the 49 poses tested my strength and flexibility. In the primary series, the practitioner holds each posture on each side for 5 long breaths and does a vinyasa in between. A vinyasa looks like a push up with an upward dog and downward dog flow.

Practicing Ashtanga yoga made me more disciplined, slimmed me down, and put me in the flow. The sequence is the exact same every time, and I didn't have to worry about following the instructor because I knew what's coming next. At the end of the 90-minute practice, I did breath work and meditation. After morning Ashtanga yoga, we would all devour fresh smoothie bowls with sliced bananas and nuts. The training was a full-day commitment - from 6 a.m. to 7 p.m. This was the schedule:

6-8AM Ashtanga Practice

8-9AM Breakfast

9-10 Anatomy

10 AM- 1 PM Ashtanga Theory

1-2 PM Lunch Break

2-4 PM Yoga Philosophy

4-5 PM Pranayama/ Meditation

5-6 PM Yin/Restorative Theory

 6-7 Yin/ Restorative Practice

In between classes, we would take breaks and drink fresh juices from the cafe in front of the shala. I quickly realized my favorite was turmeric juice. It was bright orange in the glass and had a strong, satisfying, earthy taste. I did not know what turmeric was before going to Bali. Turmeric is known for its anti-inflammatory properties. When I drank it, I could feel the juice cleansing my organs.

I was also a fan of Bali coffee; I would order it all the time. As you can imagine practicing yoga and learning all day did get tiring at times. I would order a Bali coffee from the cafe to perk me up. It was like nothing I'd ever tried before in the states. Balinese coffee was brewed by pouring hot water into a mug and then pouring a generous helping of grounds into the mug. The powdery ground coffee would mostly dissolve into the hot water, making coffee, but the leftover powder would sink to the bottom, making a pile that looked like mud. The coffee was bold, full of caffeine, and delicious. The beans were grown and roasted in Bali so the coffee was incredibly fresh as well.

I practiced Yin Yoga in the evening. Yin yoga is a type of yoga where you hold poses for three to five minutes instead of only for a few breaths like in Ashtanga. The poses are typically floor postures such as a twist lying down, a child's pose, or a forward fold.

Yin is very relaxing, but at the same time can be challenging because you sink so deeply into each pose, your limbs can start shaking. Less movement also means more time to think and reflect.

# Chapter 2

By a stroke of luck I was stable in Bali - I was neither manic nor depressed. For the most part I was joyful and at peace. I was not elated. Just content and full of awe and wonder.

One of the evenings I felt most in sync with the rhythm of life was when I watched the sunset on the beach with my Danish friend. Her name was Dakin, and for being so young, she was full of wisdom. Dakin had long blonde locks that draped down her back and always looked beautiful. The way she flowed through our yoga sequences made it seem like even the most difficult poses were simple to hold. Dankin was graceful and lovely, with bright blue eyes and an elegant smile. It surprised me that she sought out Ashtanga teacher training. Although she was elegant she had great inner strength and discipline alike.

The evening we watched the sunset together we gazed at the horizon of the ocean for over an hour. As the sun set, the thousands of clouds bunching up around the sun were set on fire. To this day, this sun set was the most memorable to me. (Besides the one I saw my uncle watching while I was in spirit soaring over him.)

The water lapped on the beach, creating a nice slow rhythm as the tide went out farther and farther. Watching that sun melt away helped me realize that I do matter and life is worth living. I told Dankin about my plans to move from Arizona to Los Angeles to live with Derrick when I got home from the yoga training.

"I hope Derrick understands how big of a deal it is that you are moving to California for him. Never forget your worth and value, Mallory. You need to do what your heart is telling you to

do, but if things change, that's ok. Always follow your heart no matter what," Dankin told me one night on the beach as the dusk faded into night and the stars started to come out.

We laid there on the sand talking about life, our hopes and dreams, and Bali. I will always treasure this moment I had with Dankin. We had only spent about a week doing yoga together, yet she cared so deeply about me and the next adventure I had on the horizon. Dankin was a sensitive, kind soul and I feel blessed to have known her for the three short weeks we spent at training.

After 200 hours of training, I passed all of my yoga tests and was now certified to teach Yin and Ashtanga yoga back in the United States. And even though the program was done, I wasn't done with Bali. I decided to spend another week scuba diving and exploring.

The next island on my list was Nusa Penida. When my yoga training ended, I hopped on the back of a local boy's scooter, and he drove me to the dock a few miles away from my hotel. There, I boarded a dinghy that motored me across a span of the Indian Ocean to Nusa Penida. The ride was smooth and short. There were other boats cruising around in the water on my way there. We docked in Nusa Penida, and I checked into my hostel and hung out on the patio. I knew I would need to rent a motor scooter if I was going to explore this island.

I walked around the few streets that made up the local town. Every other local home had its own personal Hindu temple in front of their house. There was one ATM and only a few little hole-in-the-wall restaurants. As I was walking, I saw a crowd of locals with motor scooters hanging out by a pier. I approached a few of them, asking to rent a scooter and was basically shunned. There were so many scooters available I was confused as to why none of these locals wanted to help me out. I finally gave up trying to score one and turned back to retreat to my hostel. I only got one block away when a local walked up to me and whispered he would rent me one if I met him in the alley way. I was not sure why he was acting so shady, but I was desperate for a scooter.

I walked around the block and down the alleyway, and low and behold, he had a glorious scooter that he was going to rent out to me. I started feeling pretty excited.

"Thanks so much for renting me a scooter. No one else would even pay attention to me!" I said to him, bursting with happiness.

"Shh, keep it down," he replied.

"Oh, I'm sorry. Wait, why wouldn't anyone else rent me one?" I whispered back.

"Today, holy holiday. Locals come here to Nusa Penida to celebrate from other islands, and they all need scooters. They don't want to rent them out to tourists," he said.

"That makes sense. Well, thanks for renting it to me. I want to go check out the holy cave down the road."

"Ok, here is the scooter. Meet me back in this alleyway to return it before night time."

"Thank you, yes I will! Can I take it out tomorrow, too? I'm planning on hiking Kelingking Cliff."

"Maybe. Bye. Bye!"

I hopped on the scooter and drove off to check out the cave. I did not know exactly where it was, but I knew to drive down the main street for a while. I had grown up driving four-wheelers, but this was a two-wheeled scooter. I was nervous about losing control by speeding over a loose patch of gravel. I maintained a moderate speed down the winding road to be on the safe side. I also said some Hail Marys while on the road for extra protection. I would be screwed if I fell, I was in Asia by myself. I kept driving until I passed a large monument that said "Goa Giri Putri." I turned around and parked in front of the monument, marking the cave entrance.

There were men, women and children climbing a steep flight of stairs. I followed them up and stepped up on a platform at the top. Small statues of Hindu gods lined the entrance of the cave, and I saw a man chanting in front of a large seated group of people while another man threw rice at a crowd of people around the platform. I quickly realized - this was a holy Hindu ceremony. When it was over, the crowd began to retreat deeper inside the cave.

I stepped inside the cave, which was glowing with a blueish hue, and saw a man dunking cave water on people's heads. I walked up to him, bowed my head, and he drenched me in water. It felt like a cleansing ceremony, but I didn't try to ask. I followed the crowd as we retreated deeper into the cave.

A couple of caverns in, I stopped to watch a second ceremony. The sound of chanting reverberated through the cave and a group of men and women were burning incense. I retreated to the end and made my way back out, emerging under the sun.

I was so far from home participating in a Hindu practice. I had come to Bali to take a yoga teacher training, but looking back, I realized that I was trying to find myself, and I went searching as far as the other side of the world to figure out who I was. I thought I had been blessed in that cave. But the real blessing was that God kept me safe while I was there. I did not have a mood episode and was mostly in reality.

Later, I realized that I dove into yoga training because I was so desperate to find something to believe in. As many things in life the experience was neither all good nor all bad but a mix of the two. I made some new friends, worked out, experienced another culture, and got to go scuba diving, surfing, and exploring. However, I realized that I am not comfortable repeating the opening chant to the Ashtanga Yoga practice. It includes the words "Vande Gurunam Charanaravinde", which is Sanskrit for "I bow to the lotus feet of the Supreme Guru", and "Abahu Purushakaram", which is Sanskrit for "I prostrate before the sage Patanjali."

Bowing down to anyone besides Jesus is breaking the first commandment. Deuteronomy 6:5 says, 'You shall love Yahweh your God with all your heart, with all your soul, and with all your might.' Some of the postures in yoga are positions held to offer worship to Hindu deities. I was offering up worship to other gods when I was practicing yoga.

Yoga made me feel so incredibly good. The breathing, stretching, and postures helped me to get stronger and more flexible. I always felt happier and more relaxed after yoga. This feeling after taking a yoga class became addictive. I was no longer addicted to substances but was addicted to yoga. When I realized I was worshipping other gods, it was difficult to cut the practice out of my life because I did get some benefits from yoga. But when I was doing it, I was opening myself up to other spirits. I know in my heart I can no longer practice yoga if I am to serve the Father, Son, and Holy Spirit.

1 Corinthians 10: 21-22 says 'Ye cannot drink the cup of the Lord, and the cup of demons: ye cannot partake of the table of the Lord, and of the table of demons. Or do we provoke the Lord to jealousy? Are we stronger than he?'

Cutting yoga out of my life once and for all completely disconnected me from New Age spirituality. It was the first practice that brought me into it, and the last thing that I finally cut out.

Matthew 5:29-30 says 'If your right eye causes you to stumble, pluck it out and throw it away from you. For it is more profitable for you that one of your members should perish than for your whole body to be cast into Gehenna. If your hand causes you to stumble, cut it off, and throw it away from you. For it is more profitable for you that one of your members should perish than for your whole body to be cast into Gehenna.' This verse came to mind when I once and for all finally decided to quit doing yoga.

After exploring Nusa Penida, my time in Indonesia had come to an end. I hopped on a boat back to Bali and caught a flight out after being there for a whole month. When I landed in Phoenix, I didn't waste any time. I immediately started packing to move into an apartment with Derrick.

Derrick met me in Phoenix. We rented a 15-foot U-Haul, packed it up with the furniture my dad brought back from Washington, and then hitched a 15-foot trailer onto the U-Haul truck. I drove my Subaru up on that trailer. Derrick and I took turns driving that rig until we reached our destination - Los Angeles.

My family was not happy with me moving out there with the person I hit rock bottom within Washington. We were both over a year sober, though and very dedicated to our recovery. We rented out a cute little one-bedroom apartment at a complex that had a lovely pool and hot tub. Derrick and I were engaged and in love and were over the moon to at last be together again.

Derrick was working at a small business and, at the same time, going to school for business, taking classes in the evenings. I found a job as a spa attendant at a 5-star hotel. I worked there for a few months, but I started to grow very depressed. I was cycling down after a year of mania and the high of the Bali trip.

I did pretty much every single thing my rehab program had recommended to stay sober. I was going to AA meetings regularly, I was working out, I had a job to keep me busy, and I even made a wonderful group of sober friends. I checked all of the boxes of what a sober person needs to do to be fulfilled and happy, yet I would cry my eyes out in the evenings when Derrick was in class.

I asked my sponsor for help, telling her about the daunting feelings of depression that were starting to consume me. But she did not know how to help me and simply gave me the advice to ask God to take away my depression. I prayed to God for help, but the depression did not lift. While I know it is possible for God to take away depression, I also know he works through mental health professionals such as psychiatrists and licensed therapists to help people recover from mental illness. I know praying did not hurt, but I needed medical attention to help me get out of this mood episode, but I didn't know that yet. I wish my sponsor, Derrick, or anybody at all would have recommended I go see a psychiatrist for depression. I had never seen a psychiatrist in my life, not even in rehab, so I kept on going without any professional help.

# Chapter 3

My bipolar disorder was cycling again. Months passed, and I decided to quit my job. I was not happy cleaning workout equipment and checking in snooty hotel guests at the spa gym. I knew I was meant for so much more I just did not know what exactly. I went through another identity crisis in terms of not knowing which career path to go after. TV News was out of the question - it was too cutthroat and I did not enjoy reporting on all of the negative stories. I started teaching yoga at a gym once a week, but this was not God's will for my life, and I was not using my higher intelligence on a day to day basis like I wanted to. I looked into a master's counseling program at a university in Los Angeles but was not in the headspace to start school again while battling bipolar depression.

Meanwhile, Derrick was still on antipsychotics under the care of a psychiatrist. This doctor, who believed Derrick's symptoms were solely a result of his substance use 1.5 years ago, saw he was completely stable now and took him off his medication. This caused some major troubles for Derrick and our relationship. After Derrick's psychiatrist took him off his meds, he stopped going to meetings. He fell under the delusion that he was "better" and that he did not need them. Derrick had been going to at least five meetings a week, so this was a drastic change. The meetings and medication had kept him grounded and stable. He quickly elevated into mania. He took me shopping for crystals at a massive shop in downtown Los Angeles and impulsively bought over $1,000 worth of crystals.

He said he wanted to "up-level the energy" in our apartment. He also impulsively bought a motorcycle and got his license to ride.

At night, Derrick became extremely irritable while manic and yelled very loudly at me. I was so scared of this person I never had experienced this side of him before. Even in Washington, he was extremely psychotic but never aggressive with me. One night, he was so irritable, manic and angry that he cornered me in our apartment, screaming in my face. He taunted me and said that I did "guru worship." He snatched my purse when I tried to leave, and he wouldn't let me get a hold of it. Eventually, I grabbed it from him and ran to my car with him chasing after me. I managed to drive out of the apartment complex safely and found a hotel to stay in at 2 A.M.

First thing in the morning, I called my sponsor and told her what happened. She listened without judgment and shared some kind, healing words with me. After our conversation, I knew what I had to do - break up with Derrick. I could not bear to stay with him after he betrayed me and called me those horrible names. I moved all the way out to Los Angeles to be with him, and he threw our relationship away by treating me like trash. I was not going to stick around - I knew I needed to get the hell out of Los Angeles and move back to Arizona, where my family was.

I went back to the apartment that morning and found Derrick sitting on our seafoam green couch.

"I don't know what that was last night, Derrick, but this is the third time you freaked out at me like that. I cannot let you stay here anymore. I don't want to find out what will happen next. I want to break up with you." I told him sternly.

"No, we can't break up, I'm sorry Mallory." Derrick cried out, tears welling up in his eyes. "I didn't mean those things I said; I couldn't control myself!" At this point, I knew there was something very wrong with Derrick, but I didn't realize he had a mood disorder.

I stood my ground and told him, "This is not working, please pack up all of your clothes, take your tapestries, and get out."

After everything we had been through together in Washington, doing long distance while we were in rehab, visiting each other, getting engaged and moving to Los Angeles together, I could not believe this was happening.

He did not fight me again, though. Derrick packed his bags and left our apartment. He moved back in with his parents 15 minutes away. When he left, I was lonely and afraid in that apartment. One evening, a random man knocked on my door. He had a bike with him and he reeked of weed.

"Is Derrick here?" he asked.

"No, he does NOT live here. Please do not come back." I shut the door and dead bolted it. I had a hunch that Derrick had relapsed and may have been getting high with this man. I was not sure why

Derrick gave him my address and apartment number but it made me nervous.

A couple of days later, I woke up at 2 A.M. to Derrick yelling, "Mallory, Mallory, let me in!" outside of my glass sliding bedroom door. I was so afraid. I locked myself in my bathroom and called the police.

I eventually got the guns to crack open the sliding glass door and yell, "I called the cops, Derrick, get out of here!"

The cops showed up right after he sped off on his motorcycle. I told them what was going on, and they were very kind to me. They told me I could call again if he came back.

About a week later, Derrick showed up at my apartment during the day and left a $600 crystal lamp on the porch. I saw him jump over the ledge and place it by the chair outside. I caught him doing it. This time I saw him, I felt less threatened since he wasn't showing up in the middle of the night. He told me he just left me a present to say sorry for everything. I looked at the lamp, and it was actually quite beautiful. It was turquoise and purple in a hollow square shape about 1.5 feet tall. Derrick left, and I decided to keep the crystal lamp. It cast a gorgeous light when I plugged it in.

This was not like Derrick to be so angry and irritable and to buy so many expensive things, including crystals and a motorcycle. The thought crossed my mind: maybe he is bipolar. But I still couldn't comprehend what that really meant.

After Derrick dropped off the lamp, he didn't drop by again. It was July at this point, and I only had roughly a month left on the apartment lease, which was now fully in my name, so I was responsible for paying the entire rent.

During my last month in that apartment in Los Angeles, I attended a "training" called Shamanism for Beginners. For two days, over 16 hours, I learned "basic shaman skills." This training only made my psychotic thinking worse, making me more far removed from reality and digging deeper into the world of magical thinking. During the training sessions, we banged on drums, talked about ways to access the underworld, and went on journeys in our imaginations with the "lead shaman's" guidance. We also watched the "lead shaman" communicate with a dead person's spirit, learned how to use sage to clear energy, and were initiated as "beginner shamans."

Even though I was very interested in shamanism, I felt very unsettled when the woman leading the training connected with a dead spirit. I had never been around anything like that before, and it scared me. And it didn't help going home to a lonely apartment. But I did have my kitty 'Rikki' to keep me company. Derrick had bought her for me when we were still together. He let me keep her in the break up because he was living at his parent's house and could not take care of her. Rikki kept me company, but I was very uneasy after that training.

A few more weeks passed and I got very serious about moving back to Arizona. I really wanted to put down some roots in Tucson, so I frantically began looking online at condos there. I found a newly built 900-square-foot home in the same charming little neighborhood I lived in a while at Harmony Haven Sober Living. I booked a flight to Tucson to check out the condo. I liked that it was new, had two bedrooms, and two bathrooms. I was desperate to buy it and get out of Los Angeles, so I jumped to buy the place even though I had only seen one other condo in Tucson. I made a very impulsive, manic decision. This was the biggest purchase of my life and I did it so very quickly without putting much time, thought, or research into it.

I flew back to Los Angeles after going under contract, packed up the apartment and hit the road with Rikki with a U-Haul storage trailer hitched to the back of my Subaru. It was a 2-day drive by myself and my cat all the way from Los Angeles to Tucson. Luckily, I made it and did not get a flat tire.

I was starting a new life in Tucson without Derrick and I faced this new chapter in my life as bravely as I could. I bought furniture for my condo and jumped into a new routine. I meditated every morning, then I would hop on my computer and start working on my newest idea: starting a life coaching business.

Derrick called me after I had been living in Tucson for a month. "Hello?" I answered the phone.

"Mallory, I miss you," said Derrick.

"What do you want, Derrick?" I asked.

"I need to tell you something," he said.

"Ok, what?" I replied.

"I got diagnosed with bipolar disorder."

"Oh wow, Derrick. I'm sorry to hear that." Things clicked for me a bit.

"I am so sorry for how I treated you. I was out of control and manic. My life is ruined. I am struggling so badly right now," he apologized again.

"Derrick, I thought you might be bipolar. Thanks for calling and telling me. But you need to start manifesting your new life. That's what I'm doing. I'm manifesting a life coaching business. Think about what you want and visualize it. Tell yourself every night in the mirror what you want and believe you will have it." I spoke rapidly and with enthusiasm.

"I want you, Mallory," he said.

"You might have to manifest something else, Derrick, because we are not getting back together. I will pray for you, though."

We said our goodbyes and hung up the phone.

The same week I moved to Tucson, I dropped $8,000 on a life coach business training course, and I threw myself into it. Through this course, I started my own Facebook group, created a Facebook ad to attract clients, made sales pitches for my coaching program, created engagement, held contests to get people excited, and even made sales calls with potential clients.

The training course lasted one month. Overall, I created a lot of engagement and laid a solid foundation for an online coaching business. I even got one client who paid me $50 a session that I very much enjoyed working with. But I didn't realize that I was deep into a hypomanic state while getting this business off the ground. The training course told us that we needed to "manifest" our clients by repeating phrases to ourselves in the mirror over and over again before going to sleep.

Before bed, I would look at myself and say, "Clients are coming my way, clients are coming my way." I was under the impression that I was responsible for bringing in my clients myself through these mantras. I was truly convinced that if I didn't do the mantras every single night, the business would not work. It made sense to me in my psychotic and manic brain. But in reality, all I could have done was build the business, market myself to the best of my ability, and then leave the results up to God.

It became exhausting marketing myself all day and trying to manifest money and clients every night. When I only got one client throughout the entire training course, I became frustrated. I definitely was not getting a return on my investment. Was I doing something wrong? The course ended, and I started to crash.

# Chapter 4

My motivation to keep marketing this coaching business was faltering, and I started to feel a drastic shift inside of me. I woke up one morning and it hit me like a ton of bricks that I needed to stop participating in New Age practices. I felt a very strong desire to get rid of all the crystals in my condo, throw away my yoga books, stop doing yoga, repent, and go back to church. I can't explain why I randomly woke up one morning and felt disgusted by all of the New Age stuff around my condo. The only explanation I can think of is it was divine intervention by the Holy Spirit helping me turn away from all of my sinful ways and start trusting Jesus again.

I got rid of thousands of dollars-worth of crystals. I threw out my yoga clothes. I canceled my yoga membership. I stopped burning sage in my condo. I got rid of hundreds of dollars-worth of yoga and New Age books. I started pouring over the bible, reciting verses as loudly as I could in my condo. I grew severely depressed. I went to church and confessed to the priest I had been involved in New Age spirituality. I was sobbing in confession, but the father had no idea what I was talking about and even asked me if I was upset because I had gotten an abortion. He didn't understand what I was going through and he did not know what the New Age was. But he didn't need to because Jesus did. Jesus is who I was there to talk to anyways. I knew Jesus could rescue me from Satan and the New Age.

Turning away from the New Age and dealing with the worst bipolar depression I had ever experienced in my life was no easy task. I was completely alone in my condo, my coaching business collapsed, and all of the beliefs I had for the past two years came crashing down. I would sob all day long and could hardly shower or feed myself. I talked to my mom, and she told me she thought I needed serious help. She told me my uncle knew a psychiatrist in Phoenix who might be able to help.

The last thing I wanted to admit was that I needed help yet AGAIN. I tried getting myself together. I mustered up all of the strength I had to apply for jobs. This is when things began to get even worse. Instead of being depressed OR manic, I was rapid cycling again between racing thoughts, bursts of energy, shopping impulsively, drivingly recklessly, and feeling foggy, suicidal, and weighed down like a rock. I would alternate between up and down very frequently throughout one day. I started to believe I was going crazy again. I was scared that this was happening because I was 100% sober this time. It started to dawn on me that I could not control my moods, thoughts, or actions, and I started fearing for my life. I told my mom what was happening, and this time, she insisted I drive to Phoenix to see this doctor.

When I thought back to what happened in my Los Angeles apartment when a manic Derrick screamed at me, I started to have pity for him. I realized he really did not have any control over what he was doing. I called him before I made the trip to Phoenix.

"Hello?" answered Derrick.

"Derrick, I have to tell you some things." First, all of the New Age spiritual things we believed in are evil. You need to turn to Jesus; he is the only one who can save us."

"Ok, I'm listening," said Derrick.

"Next, I want to forgive you for how you treated me at the apartment. I now understand you had absolutely no control over yourself. I think I am bipolar, too, and I'm having episodes where I get so irritable and have crazy bursts of energy. But then the next moment, I want to kill myself." I was shouting into the phone, deep in the middle of a mood episode.

"Mallory, I am so sorry you are going through this. I know exactly what that feels like. It is so hard to be so out of control. I am doing better now, though. I have been sober for two months now and am taking medication again. Medication will help you, Mallory!" said Derrick.

"Yes, I am going to see a psychiatrist in Phoenix. Thank you so much for answering my call. I know we have not spoken in a while. I am going through a very difficult time, and you're the only person I know who has been through this. Pray for me." I pleaded.

"I will, Mallory. Call me if you need to talk to a friend. Please call for support, especially when you are feeling suicidal." We wrapped up the call and then hung up.

The next morning, I packed up what I needed for a couple of weeks and loaded up my car with Rikki. I called the doctor's office to schedule an appointment. The phone rang 10 times, and no one answered. At the end, there was an answering machine saying I needed to leave a message if I wanted to get on the waiting list. I did not realize how difficult it was going to be to get an appointment with this doctor. I called again and again with no luck each time. I hung up without leaving a message. I did not want to get on a waiting list. I needed to get in right away!

I called my uncle to tell him I was not having any luck scheduling an appointment. He told me I needed to "work the system." "Leave a message, Mallory. Call back every morning right away when they open to see if there were any cancellations," he said.

I was stunned that it was so hard to see this doctor. I called back and left a message saying I desperately needed an appointment. I locked up my condo and hit the road for Phoenix.

When I made it to my mom's house I settled in and let Rikki out in my room. I was very anxious and on edge about seeing the doctor. I called again and again with no luck. The next morning, I called right away at 8 A.M. when they opened. No one answered. I called a second time.

BINGO! A lady picked up. I told her I needed to get in to see the doctor immediately and to PLEASE let me know if they had any cancellations. She seemed annoyed, but she did acknowledge me so

I was hopeful. She said she put me on the list and she would call if anything opened up.

The rest of the morning I did not let go of my phone for a moment. The doctor's office called me at 11:45 A.M. and told me if I could get to the office in 45 minutes, I could see the doctor. I told them I would be there and immediately jumped into my car.

I checked in when I arrived and waited in the waiting room for a while. The secretary let me go to the back when Dr. Drake was ready to see me.

Dr. Drake looked like he was in his 50's. He was tall, about 6'3'', had black hair and a black beard, and smelled fresh, like he had just gotten out of the shower. He had me step up onto a scale and he recorded my weight on his chart. He walked me back to his office, where we both took a seat.

"What has been going on with you, Mallory?" Dr. Drake asked.

"I have been going through a very difficult time, Dr. Drake," I replied. "I cannot control myself. My thoughts race so quickly that I cannot even keep up with what I am thinking. It scares me how fast I think. I get so much energy and get in the car and drive recklessly. I've driven the wrong way down the street. I even hallucinated and saw a swirly black vortex when I was driving and it blocked my view of the road. I believe God's wrath is upon me for sinning. After the burst of energy, I get terribly depressed. I feel so hopeless like I cannot go on, and I think about killing myself frequently. I go up and down five to six times throughout the day. I feel like I am crazy. I have felt high energy and depressed, but not six times, switching in one day. I don't know what to do. Can you PLEASE help me? Do you think I have bipolar disorder?"

Dr. Drake took notes and then looked up from the notepad. "Yes, you do have bipolar disorder. Everything you described is mania and depression with psychotic features, which explains the hallucinations. I am going to get you started on a few different medications. We will start with 25 mg of Lamotrigine, which is a very effective mood stabilizer. I will also prescribe 25 mg of Latuda, which is an antipsychotic, and 150 mg of Oxcarbazepine, which also has mood-stabilizing effects. There is one thing about the Lamotrigine." Dr. Drake's voice shifted to a more serious tone. "Some people get a deadly rash when they take it. This side effect is called Stevens-Johnson's syndrome. It is extremely rare, though."

Dr. Drake turned around and pulled up Google on his computer. He typed in Stevens-Johnsons syndrome and pulled up some images - photos of large red boils and, in some cases, skin peeling off people's bones.

"If you get a rash on your skin, call me immediately. You probably won't, but just in case you do, I will need to prescribe you steroids to counteract the rash. If the rash is not caught in time, you can lose your skin and die."

I was taken aback by this information. "OK, but it's very rare, right? You think this medication will help me?" I was so terribly naive at this point. I had no idea how difficult it is for a person newly diagnosed with bipolar disorder to stabilize on the right combination of meds.

"Yes, it is rare, but be on the lookout just in case," he replied.

He ripped the prescriptions off his notepad and gave them to me. "Good luck, Mallory; go ahead and schedule your next appointment at the front desk. I will need to see you again soon."

I scheduled my appointment for a month out and left Dr. Drake's office. I got my prescriptions filled right away and began taking the medication as prescribed over the next week. But the pills made me feel very sick. I experienced everything from blurred vision, hallucinations, to heart palpitations, racing thoughts, psychotic thinking, existential religious thoughts, insomnia, and sexual arousal, and yes, I did get the deadly rash.

# Chapter 5

It was a Sunday morning, and I was putting on my dress for church when my leg became very itchy. I looked down and saw red bumps, each the size of a nickel, all up and down my legs. This was very concerning. I also saw them on my neck, chest, and even a few on my chin. *Holy moly, is this the deadly rash Dr. Drake was talking about?* Panic washed over me, and my body went cold. I did not want to die an agonizing death with my skin peeling off my bones. I couldn't call Dr. Drake fast enough and left an urgent message, telling him I had a severe rash all over my skin. I was not sure if he was going to get the message. I was scared. Less than 5 minutes later, I got a call from Dr. Drake. I couldn't believe he was getting back to me on a Sunday!

"Mallory, I am calling in a prescription of oral steroids for you. You need to begin taking them today. You have Steven-Johnson's Syndrome. For some reason, you are allergic to Lamotrigine; this is so rare. You need to stop taking it immediately. If you take steroids, you will be fine, and the rash will go away." Dr. Drake urged.

"Ok, thank you, Dr. Drake," I replied and hung up. I was speechless. *Why in the world did I have this extremely rare allergic reaction?* I thought to myself, *probably because I am a redhead.*

I picked up the steroids, packed my car with Rikki, and drove back to Tucson. I knew how mentally ill I was, but I felt like a child again, staying with my mom. I wanted to see if I could make it to

Tucson by myself for a few more weeks before my next appointment with Dr. Drake.

I started the steroids when I got back to Tucson. I was on them for three days, and then one day, I forgot to take my morning and afternoon doses. So, I decided to take all four steroid pills in the afternoon before my AA meeting. While sitting in my chair at the meeting, I started to "come up" on those steroids. Later, I found out that oral steroids taken by someone with bipolar disorder can make them manic - something that Dr. Drake did not warn me about. The feeling was so intense it felt like a rush. I ran out of the meeting and a man who was walking in late saw me freaking out in the parking lot and talked to me for 15 minutes to help ground me. I got in the car, left the AA meeting, and started driving back to my condo. I called Derrick to tell him what happened.

"I'm not doing too well, Derrick. I had a huge manic rush after taking those steroids for my deadly rash. Now, I am crashing hard. I want to kill myself. I can't keep going up and down like this and having these extreme side effects from the meds. I can hardly take it anymore." My voice filled with panic.

"I get it, Mallory. There's nothing I can say to make things better besides that I understand what you are going through. You just gotta keep riding it out until you find the right meds," he told me.

Talking to Derrick gave me strength. These ups and downs were horrible and I was tired of doing all of this. But I kept going.

I finished the steroids, and the rash went away. The bipolar roller coaster continued as Dr. Drake tweaked my medications and started increasing my doses. One night, when I was trying to fall asleep, my heart started racing, beating so hard in my chest that I bolted up from the bed. My heart was beating the hardest it ever had in my entire life. *I am having a heart attack*; I panicked inside my head. I started gasping for air - I couldn't get enough oxygen to my lungs - and I started hyperventilating.

I called 911 and screamed into the phone that I was having a heart attack. When the paramedics showed up at my door, I was starting to calm down. I told them that I thought I was having a heart attack. They said I was having a panic attack and offered to bring me to the hospital. I declined to get in the ambulance. I knew that bill would be thousands of dollars. They took my vitals and told me I was going to be fine. I thanked them, and they left.

That night, demons haunted me in my room. It felt like Satan had sent them to mock me and make fun of me for having my panic attack. I could feel their presence surrounding me and could visualize one in particular with the head of a ram. I stared at the crucifix hanging in my room as I blasted Christian screamo music in my headphones and balled my eyes out. I was caught in the depths of mental and spiritual suffering. Jesus was the only person who truly understood the darkness I was going through. I felt angry at God for putting me through so much mental anguish. But when I looked at that cross, I knew Jesus understood because God allowed him to be crucified just like God allowed me to have bipolar disorder. That night, I gained my strength, and Christ redeemed me for everything - the New Age practices, the substance use, and every other sin I had committed in my life up until this point. I did not call my mom or Derrick to tell them about the panic attack, 911, or the demons haunting me. I just spent the night with Jesus.

When I woke up the next morning I called Derrick and told him about what happened. Over the next few weeks, I leaned on Derrick for support as I continued to live in bipolar hell. We grew very close again, and I asked him to move into my condo with me. Weeks later, he packed up his stuff and jumped on a plane from Los Angeles to Tucson. My family was disappointed that we moved back in together again. But they didn't understand how much support I got from Derrick. I drove to Phoenix a few more times as Dr. Drake worked with me to adjust my meds. Even though Derrick was living with me, I was still extremely unstable.

Derrick and I worked hard to find new jobs. Derrick applied for software developer positions, and I applied to basically anything that looked interesting. I was hired as a sales representative at a company. I worked there for one week and quit. I was too unstable and lacked the concentration to hold down a 9 to 5 desk job.

It felt like my depression was eating me alive. I wasn't just chemically depressed. I was also depressed about the trajectory of my life. I felt like I did in Los Angeles, but even worse off since my mood was completely out of control. I tried to go on a walk, ride my bike, get sunshine, and I even drank a smoothie that was supposed to help fight depression. Nothing worked. The only thing that slightly helped was talking to my support system which consisted of Derrick, my mom, and an occasional chat with one of my siblings, or dad. I became so depressed one night that I couldn't stop thinking about dying. Derrick called 911 because he couldn't help me. I started throwing up when the paramedics, and the mental health officer walked into my condo. I quickly packed an overnight bag, and the mental health officer took me to a crisis center.

When I walked inside the crises center, a man who looked like he might have been homeless asked me what I was doing there. All I told him was, "I want to go to heaven." At that point, I felt like I was done with Earth. There was nothing left for me here. The man offered me a cigar. I took him up on the offer and slid the cigar into my bag, and he walked out of the door and left.

I spent three nights at the crisis center. I met other people with severe mental health problems and became friends with them. One offered me cigarettes and smoked them with me outside. This helped a little. I saw a social worker and a psychiatric nurse practitioner. While staying there, I heard about an antidepressant called Wellbutrin. I called Dr. Drake and let him know I was admitted into a crisis center because my depression got so bad, and I asked him if Wellbutrin could help me. He went ahead and wrote me a prescription, but the psychiatric nurse practitioner wasn't happy about it.

"It could help. But it could also make you extremely anxious," she told me.

I started my first dose and got discharged from the crisis center. Derrick picked me up and brought me back to the condo.

"I'm hoping this new medication will help," I told him. I had been through so much. I wasn't sure if I had any fight left in me. That night, I slept fine. But the next night, I didn't sleep a wink.

In the morning, the anxiety started creeping in. My appetite was not very good either. I called my uncle. He gave me the advice to keep taking the medication, and the anxiety and insomnia might go away. So, I took another dose. My anxiety kicked up about 10 more gears. I was full-blown, out of my seat, unable to think straight, racing thoughts, racing heart, blood coursing through my veins, manic. This was the worst mania I had ever experienced in my entire life.

I felt desperate to relapse. I was crawling out of my skin and could hardly bear to be alive. I wanted to drink to make it better. I walked down the stairs of my condo to go to the gas station and buy some liquor. Derrick stopped me.

"Mallory, if you do this, it will help temporarily, but then it will get worse. I wouldn't drink if I were you. Trust me, I drank, and it took me 6 months to finally stop again," he warned me.

I knew he was right. I was just going to have to suffer. I bought a pack of the gold American Spirit cigarettes instead, chain-smoking them one after another for the rest of the day. But I was barely hanging on. I called my doctor and begged him for some Ativan, a narcotic that calms anxiety. He refused to prescribe it to me and instead gave me Trazodone, a non-narcotic sleep medication. I took a shower to attempt to calm myself and popped my nighttime meds, including a Trazadone this time, begging God to let me sleep. I had been awake and manic for 3 days straight at this point.

When Derrick and I laid down in bed that night, it took him 15 minutes to fall asleep but I was wide awake, tossing and turning. The only thing I could think of was buying a plane ticket to San Francisco and jumping off the Golden Gate Bridge. I imagined how freeing it would feel to let go of the rail and plunge to my death. I would not mind dying in the ocean. *I want to kill myself. I need to kill myself. This needs to end once and for all.*

I frantically got out of bed. I thought about calling 911 but decided that was not going to work. I needed help immediately. I couldn't wait for them to get here.

"Derrick, wake up!" I screamed. "Take me to the ER, NOW!"

We got in the car, and he sped down the highway to the nearest hospital. He dropped me off, and I flew out of the car without even saying bye to him.

I ran through the hospital's sliding doors and checked myself in. A nurse put me in a dark, isolated room with cold stone walls. She asked me why I was in the ER.

"I am having the worst manic episode of my life, and I desperately want to kill myself," spitting the words out of my mouth.

She barely said a word to me and left. She shut me in the isolated room. It was freezing cold, and there was one chair in the center of the room. The door leading to the hallway had a window in it.

I started banging my head against the stone-cold wall to make the racing thoughts stop. I could not handle what was going on inside of my head.

A nurse saw me, opened the door and yelled at me. "You need to stop that, or we will have to restrain you to that chair!"

My vision started getting blurry, and a man in scrubs walked into my dark room and gave me a shot. He said it was full of antipsychotics and that it should help.

I calmed down a tiny bit and ended up sitting in a chair, waiting for five hours to be seen by a doctor. Finally, one walked in around six in the morning and asked me a few questions. He told me to stop taking the Wellbutrin and that he was going to release me now. I was so confused. Weren't they going to give me some *real* help?

Derrick came and picked me up. The shot did help a little bit, but I still felt extremely manic. It was better than nothing, but in my opinion, I should've been prescribed Klonopin, a narcotic medication that helps reduce anxiety and mania.

I called Dr. Drake to tell him what happened. At last, he prescribed me the medication that would bring back my sanity: Lithium. A few months passed, and I stabilized on the Lithium combined with the Latuda. It was the magic cocktail that made my brain function. I made the decision to apply to graduate school and I got accepted. I started pursuing a career in counseling only a few months after stabilizing. I thought maybe, just maybe, if I got this degree, I could help others out there struggling with bipolar disorder. It was the beginning of my new journey.

The addiction, bipolar trauma, and spiritual warfare I went through took its toll on me, but the Holy Spirit inside of me gave me the strength to never give up.

Instead of resorting to suicide, I went to the hospital. Instead of drinking, I played the tape through. Instead of isolating, I reached out to my support system. Only by the grace of God did I make it out of the bipolar flames alive.

New Age spirituality was a very dangerous path to go down for me because it made my psychosis so much worse. Magical thinking in shamanism, playing God by trying to "manifest" my life, worshiping false gods through yoga, and reading endless New Age articles on the internet brought me much further down a rabbit hole leading to spiritual psychosis. I will be forever grateful for escaping the New Age through divine intervention.

'For all have sinned, and fall short of the glory of God; being justified freely by his grace through the redemption that is in Christ Jesus.' Romans 3:23-24.